IMMERSIVE MENTORING

MARISA **PIÑEIRO**

LEADERSHIP IS WRITTEN WITH C

CORE OF THE HEART, THE STRENGTH TO UNDERSTAND AND SHOW THAT THERE ARE NO LIMITS

amazon kindle

MARISA PIÑEIRO

MARISA PIÑEIRO

LEADERSHIP IS WRITTEN WITH C

Core of the heart, the strength to understand and show that there are no limits

MARISA PIÑEIRO

Leadership is written with C

Core of the heart, the strength to understand and show that there are no limits

Published by Marisa Piñeiro

Amazon Kindle

amazon
kindle

V. 44.895

Amazon Paperback ISBN **979-887-15651-3-1**

Amazon Hardcover ISBN **979-887-15656-2-9**

First edition Spanish @2020

First edition English @2023

I dedicate this book to all women.

And to their hearts!

INDEX

11

Preface

When I received the draft of Marisa's first book, lovingly inviting me to write the prologue, I knew that her intention was to demonstrate that there are no limits to achieving goals in life if you work with your heart. That is what Marisa wants to convey.

I have known her for many years, and I always saw her as woman determined to get out of every circumstance flawlessly.

Low profile, lover of interdisciplinary, leader of eclectic teams, curious and with a unique ability to learn.

A tireless worker in her two roles, selfless mother of Calita and a mother of heart to her collaborators. Many times, I wanted to know who her mentors were, beside her parents, and her secret to advance in her career and not be intimidated by each challenge.

I loved reading that she divided the book into three parts that can guide a woman to grow, and that the main secret is to work with genuine feelings as they are essential for generating trust and building strong bonds in every context.

I do not want to spoil the contents of the book, but I do want to ensure that Marisa clearly describes to us what it means to lead with the letter C as in core of the heart. I loved that she was able to weave chapter after chapter with various needed skills that start with the letter C. She knows that Communication is my heart.

Marisa is very creative when designing a strategic plan, presented in an especially simple way where she shares all her knowledge and experience.

Writing a preface is adding another look at the author's point of view, because in Marisa's work I have managed to read myself. When you read, you establish a nice conversation with the writer.

There are thousands of leadership books and courses, but rarely have I seen material so oriented toward women.

As vice president of the Argentine Forum of Executive Women (FAME), I greatly value that one of its members can express her desire for inclusion and gender equality as she has done.

16

I hope you can see what will happen in a few years, I feel that with each chapter you can write hundreds of pages and I fully trust that you will invite readers to project themselves without limitations.

How necessary it is to have someone help us reflect, without installed models, limiting beliefs or biases so that our potential arises!

Marisa, your heart has always been immensely empathetic and generous, I hope this book helps many women, and I want to see you put it into action, just as you invite us to do in the third part.

I wish you the best, thank you for letting me walk by your side.

Alejandra Brandolini
President ABCOM
Vice President of FAME
PR Council Secretary

Dedication and Acknowledgments

I dedicate this book to all the brave and strong women in my family, my mother Irma, my aunt Nelly and my first cousin Marsale, as well as to my goddaughter Belencita who learned something from these women, also to my close friends, who I cannot name one by one because fortunately life gave me great and many, many dear friends, that I admire, that I love and that I value. I add my special dedication to my daughter, Candelaria, "Cala", the light of my eyes, to whom I wish that reading this book will accompany her and help her in some journeys of her life. I want to honor the memory and values of my parents Luis Piñeiro and Irma Mercedes Pérez, who have given me the joy of being the best parents and role models I had in my life. I value their love, humility, perseverance and especially their inspiration towards my "C", the core of my Heart.

I have many thanks to do, to everyone who helped in one way or another, to my mentees, who planted this idea when it did not exist among my goals. To my colleagues, with whom I shared many of the experiences mentioned in this book. To the leaders who were an example of integrity, capacity and openness, such as Alejandro Harrison and Horacio Moldavsky. To the person I met on the public and political level and who taught me that you can fight and deliver knowledge and experiences regardless of party flags, an extraordinary person that I am grateful for having crossed my path, Eng. Hernán Lombardi. To my mentors, editors, and collaborators, who encouraged me to write, are the ones who often believe in me more than I do myself. I especially want to thank each and every one of us who make up the ÁGORA GLOBAL network, that tribe that added a fundamental flame to me at this stage of my life and my career.

Leadership is not a magnetic personality. It's not about 'making friends' and influencing people. Leadership is about raising sights higher, raising people's performance to the standard of their potential, and building personalities beyond their personal limitations.

Peter Drucker

If your actions inspire others to dream more, learn more, do more, and become more, you are a leader.

John Quincy Adams

"There is a world of difference between compliance and commitment. A committed person provides energy, passion and enthusiasm that cannot be generated no matter how accomplished he or she is."

Effective leadership is comprised of both substance and form, a clarity of purpose of what one wants to be as a leader, and the ability to execute the roles of Visionary, Tactician, Facilitator, and Contributor. Only through this integration of Essence and Form can a leader inspire others to give of all their energy, creativity and talent.

The current business climate requires leaders who are models of integration, leaders who are excited about the possibilities of leadership. For them, leadership is being of service to others. And despite the many challenges they face, effective leaders demonstrate a deep energy, contagious excitement, and eternal hope about the future that inspires those around them.

Marisa

Introduction

The first thing I have to tell you is that I am very happy that my book has reached your hands, since the first goal it has is to share lived experiences, some assertive and others not so much, that can help you on your path of professional development so you can reach that place you want and deserve.

I am not the first and I will not be the last, but at 50 years old I have traveled a "professional career", we call it a career, I keep thinking about the term, where we run, right? Who runs us? Why do we choose to run? A topic that I will address in some passage of the book, but first I tell you that I did run, in all my years working in different executive functions.

My journey begins as a Partner of an Accounting, Tax and Business Consulting Firm, continues as Director of Human Resources first at the local level then at the regional level, passing through the position of Director of Operations until having held the position of General Manager, in a fairly masculine industry and in decades where the role of women was neither promoted, nor developed, nor supported. It seems like a rare thing to see a woman get to that place and do a good job. That is what most caught the attention of other professional women, friends, colleagues, but above all it aroused the amazement and admiration of my mentees in different programs in which I collaborated; I can mention the experience of *"shadow week"* or the walks and one-on-one meetings that remain from the beautiful relationships that are generated in the process. And they were also part of the astonishment, those who invited me to write this book, which was born a few years ago, but was waiting in a drawer while I tried to find its essence and which after discovering it one early morning not many nights ago, achieved its final kick with the drive, energy and help of one of my mentors.

That's how I embarked on this beautiful new challenge of writing my book, which today allows me to share with you, learnings that I hope will be useful to you and mistakes that I hope will become lessons. In addition to knowing a little about what women who occupy executive positions feel and how we make that role compatible with all the others of daughter, mother, partner, friend, colleague, student, neighbor, citizen, and so on an extensive list of roles could go on...

I invite you to travel through the different chapters. In the first part I seek to explain the enablers that every woman must ensure she has or develops to become an excellent leader; In the second part I describe in an experiential and colloquial way, each of the dozen skills that, in my opinion, are necessary for a woman to be able to perform in a management or executive role. Finally, in part three, I'm dedicated to putting everything into action!

Book Genesis

To begin reading, I want to tell you how this book was born and for that I think it is important to share with you a little of my story, so that you know me, and it is easy for you to understand each of my experiences.

At the time of finishing writing this book I am 50 years old, I am an only child, although life gave me a sister and a lot of beautiful friends. I have an only daughter, although my desire was to have three or more children.

I studied Economic Sciences at a public university while working during my degree and I dedicated many hours to learning and working on the practice of the academic knowledge that the university environment offered me.

My parents, from working middle class, always instilled in me that the greatest inheritance they were going to leave me were values, culture and training and everything they did and sustained was and is aligned in that sense.

My corporate career in the media industry began almost by chance, when I arrived at an interview with Horacio Moldavsky, CFO of PRAMER, a company that had been purchased by an American group. I arrived recommended by a manager from KPMG, the company's external auditors, who found a great disorder in the labor, pension and human resources areas. I had met them in a work room at the WEATHERFORD ENTERRA company, where they worked on the annual audit, and I advised the CEO in the labor, pension and HR areas.

I was always very restless, curious and extremely self-demanding. At that time, I was an independent professional, I had become a partner in the studio where I worked throughout my university career and served clients from various industries. I managed my time, had the most varied responsibilities and designed each of my days. I was almost convinced that I had found my passion!

I start by advising PRAMER; as another client in my portfolio, and for approximately 3 years, I resisted joining the company's payroll, since the idea of working in the same industry, in a single business and spending at least 8 hours in the same place made me think I was going to get bored. Of course, none of that happened, the time came when the growth of the business demanded the need to create a human resources department and they offered me to take charge of the *startup* of the area, occupying the position of director, a challenge that I loved and that I couldn't resist!

From there, I entered the most exciting corporate career that I would have never imagined a few years back.

Although for a while I continued to maintain my two roles, as partner of the studio and HR director of PRAMER, the fact that I am very committed and involved in everything, made me have to choose, since I was working an average of between 15 and 16 hours a day, a situation that put my health to the limit. That's when I decided to put myself in *standby* to my participation in the study and fully dedicate myself to the new challenge!

For that, I completed a master's degree in Strategic Human Resources Management, I needed to put an academic foundation to what was beginning to be a new passion for me, which was added to the numbers, since now I had discovered that people were also part of my passion.

Upon accepting the proposal, one of my conditions was to participate in the small board of directors, where the progress of business was decided, since this bridge between numbers and people was what really began to challenge me in a fascinating way.

During my years as an executive, I joined the

Voces Vitales mentoring program[1], to help younger women who were beginning to navigate this world, which was putting some difficult moments in my path to endure.

This is how I meet different women, beautiful people that I had the pleasure of mentoring, an activity I did from my heart through sharing my own experience. Therefore, the way I found to work on the skills that I considered should be applied in each situation, challenge, moment that they were going through or had to go through, was by telling my own anecdotes, each of them with lessons that predisposed to learning. In addition to being an effective medium, it also allowed us to get to know each other better and cultivate a bond that began a long time ago and continues to this day.

Several years ago, I began to travel the wonderful path of writing the first notes of this book, but I abandoned it for a long period, due to work commitments that did not leave me free time for this space. Obviously, the idea had not matured in

---

[1] Vital Voices Global Partnership is an American, 501, nonprofit, nongovernmental international organization that works with women leaders in the areas of economic empowerment, women's political participation, and human rights. The organization is headquartered in Washington, D.C. Foundation: March 31, 1999

me until it began to be present in my thoughts a little less than a year ago, and one morning I woke up with the title spinning around in my head. By the way, I had been dreaming about the *skills* that I wanted to develop in the book and when I reviewed them one by one, they all started with the letter "C". That's how I woke up saying 'I know! The title of the book will be Leadership is written with C!' for this iteration of all the skills starting with the same letter C, but also because passion is fundamental in my leadership style, so I associated passion with the core of our bodies, our hearts, and that is how the title of this book came about!

This is how each of these chapters are born, which I invite you to go through and enjoy, explaining enablers and skills that I consider fundamental, telling you my anecdotes and reflecting together on findings, teachings and rich experiences to take with you in your backpack. I hope that they serve you in many moments when that situation that is difficult to face arises, in addition to leaving questions for you to ask yourself, that help you explore yourself and develop the leader in you.

I invite you to delight each section, each part of this book. I am sure that it will help you become a great leader and in case it reaches you already being one, it will also provide valid seasonings to cope with those situations that are sometimes difficult to go through.

Enjoy it!

FIRST PART

ENABLERS

I have learned that people will forget what you said, they will forget what you did, but they will never forget how you made them feel.

Maya Angelou

What is an enabler?

How to start a female leadership book? Perhaps mentioning all the skills that we must develop and train? Or is there a previous step that takes place in a few seconds called: deciding to move forward?

Yes, in a few seconds one can make a decision, and then it will surely take many years and perhaps a lifetime to complete the chosen path.

I call this enabling, opening the way, providing us with what we need for our lives. Businesses need authorizations to trade and operate, that is, they must comply with certain rules that are required so that the operation between a supplier of products and/or services can fulfill a client. There are all kinds of qualifications, however, my purpose is to describe the qualifications that we must develop to feel safe, complete, with the desire to move forward, without fear of making mistakes, without vertigo, without fear or at least the minimum necessary.

Let's start by saying that incorporating women in different executive and operational roles, in any public-private organization, state, NGOs, and all types of for-profit or non-profit groups, adds an important particularity, a look and an analysis that leaves a positive impact in the results, definitely an important added value.

I like debate and mixed teams, I have had the opportunity to work with men, I have participated in all-male boards, I have had bosses, I have also led them, I have had mentors and I love diversity, what I want to highlight is that men were able to occupy places that have not been easy for women to reach. So, because of my life experience, my professional career, and having worked on projects with other executive women, with whom I have exchanged ideas and experiences, today I want to share everything I know, which in some way must have been useful to me and can serve you dear reader. At least I want to leave an idea, as complete as possible, of where I think things that can help you can happen.

The beginnings of my career

First of all, I want to tell you that in my life, **knowledge enabled me to begin**, I am a public accountant and graduate in administration, and I have always worked, since I started studying. Tenacity and persistence helped me develop commitment, courage, and confidence, all of which allowed me to occupy the role of partner in the studio where I was working while studying. That was the first milestone in my professional career.

At that time, after graduating with honors, I participated in a Y.P. program (Young Professionals) of an oil company, who after going through several instances of evaluations and a variety of tests and interviews, was selected for the position of head of taxes and pension aspects. My surprise was great when they informed me about the hiring conditions, salary and benefits since, at the time of telling me the figure, it turned out to be six times the salary I received in the accounting firm! Which I managed completely and had been doing for a long time. That's where I discover that the experience I had purchased was much more expensive than I could imagine. I was happy in the

37

studio where I worked, we shared a wide portfolio of clients, I loved the versatility of managing many industries, diverse contexts, different problems, and meeting business owners with varied styles. As I mentioned at the beginning of this book, I had a vision, wrong or closed, that made me think that, if I joined a company, organization or corporation, I would get bored of being in a single business, a single industry and structure, but the events showed me in the future that that vision would change completely.

While I was a partner in the studio, they call me as an advisor for a media company called PRAMER.

For those who do not know it, PRAMER was founded in 1993 by the media group that had Radio América and América TV and was later acquired by Liberty Global, who years later, together with MGM Latin America, formed Chello Media, Latin America. In 2016 it changed its name to AMC Networks Latin America, after Liberty Global sold Chello Media to AMC Networks.

Well, you will have seen that, if I went all this way, I never really had a chance to get bored, on

38

the contrary, fortunately I never stopped learning.

This PRAMER company had as auditors, one of the *Big Four,* KPMG (they were called *Big Six,* to the six largest global audit and consulting firms, but as Price Waterhouse merged with Coopers & Lybrand to form PricewaterhouseCoopers, the Big Five remained together with KPMG, Deloitte, Arthur Andersen, and Ernest & Young; then they were *Big Four* because Arthur Andersen was unable to continue operating as a result of the Enron case).

The challenge that was presented to me was that KPMG promptly informed PRAMER that it was not going to sign the balance sheet until the company repaired a series of irregularities regarding labor accounts, pension tax levels, issues regarding salary settlement and union issues. Because the firm KPMG was the company's external auditor, there was a clear conflict of interest to provide other audit and advisory services, which is why the company hired me to develop a report, which I carried out and also decided to prepare a report of recommendations for the company with a focus on shedding light on the reasons that had led them to such a situation, so that they do not again incur the same irregularities that had given rise to this problem.

The KPMG team contacted me when they found out that the recommendations were my own. Valuing my knowledge (a great enabler), they suggested to the company's management that they hire me to accompany them in the implementation of the recommendations presented in my report, on which they agreed one hundred percent. Of course, I accept the interesting proposal, and this is how I begin my journey in the media industry.

The company is sold again to another American group in this case LIBERTY Global. I had already started doing a postgraduate degree in labor law, in which I had to do a leveling up to be on par with the students who came from being law students, when I came from the world of numbers, and I finished it with learnings of a lot of added value in the year 2000.

In 2001 I became a mother, a moment in my life full of great happiness because I had been trying to get pregnant for many years, I had to beg, and this gave me strength to continue, because my profession made me very happy, and I also wanted

40

to give many things to my daughter.

In 2003, the company's human resources role began to have another importance and management need, and I was offered the position of Senior Vice President of Human Resources. At that time, I began training in a master's degree in strategic management, *(I repeat, always knowledge, doing, solving activities are enablers to move forward)*, which I completed years later with a postgraduate degree in management, two IAE executive programs, one the PERH (Human Resources Executive Program), and the other the PDD (Management Development Program).

Throughout my career I improved, not only due to the need to acquire new knowledge, but because of the value that it added to my performance. Over the years I added the English language, highly necessary for all types of negotiations and business analysis in the global world.

¿Why am I telling you all this? To understand that many skills became enablers to be able to continue, especially when in 2009 I suffered the loss of my partner due to a devastating cancer, something unexpected, a personal challenge of

41

tremendous impact. Sometimes I don't know where I got the strength to get up so many times, and that's why this book exists, to share the path and help many women.

I divided the book into 3 parts, in the first I talk about enablers, necessary and critical to move forward, then I bring you a second section that includes 12 skills that help us develop and allow us to have that battery necessary to occupy and assume the role of leader; and finally, I make a call to action.

I identify as enablers five aspects to develop, which are: deciding to move forward, knowing how to sell, knowing how to negotiate, knowing about finances, and developing networks and links.

No matter how much we put our core, charisma, confidence, cooperation, courage, commitment, consistency, corpus *(and soul!)*, cognition (a lot!), communication (key), criterion, and coherence; If we cannot decide or we do not know how to sell or we find it difficult to negotiate or we do not get along well with finances and we do not build networks, the path will be as difficult as swimming in sand.

It is not necessary to be a ten to advance, but we cannot achieve a delay in any of the aforementioned areas, we must aim for a minimum of 7.

1. DECIDE Conviction / Determination

Pursuing a goal, with full confidence that you are on the right path despite everyone looking at you with a strange face, that's what I call conviction!

I want to go deeper into how to make a decision.... This is when a mentee opens their eyes expecting to hear a great encyclopedia of messages.... And I simply ask them, do you want me to explain to you how to make a decision? Well, it is done by DECIDING! Making a decision takes ten seconds, please! Whether it's studying, grabbing that book that we put on the nightstand to read a long time ago, calling whoever we want, doing gymnastics, eating a nutritious and healthy diet for our body, having lunch with a relative, going to the doctor, reading our company's balance sheets many times, starting a new career and hundreds of activities that we do every year, or rather, thousands! We make thousands of decisions every year of our lives, from the simplest to the most difficult.

I learned that to grow you have to stop procrastinating and you have to make decisions...every day. It is a training; you have to exercise as much as you can to do it more and more assertively.

But... what if I'm wrong? Well, if one makes a mistake in the decision, then things will be adjusted, THEN THEY WILL BE CHANGED! But nothing will break along the way.

Deciding is to start the car, then you can go forward or backwards, but if the machine doesn't start, we will stay in the same place as always, it's that simple.

Make decisions, without fear of making mistakes. Erring is part of the path, let's not believe that we are perfect and that we cannot make mistakes, right? There are many women who have courage, but find it difficult to make decisions, and others who do make decisions, but are not capable of moving forward and putting those decisions into action. A car does not run only on gasoline, it also needs wheels, and hundreds of mechanisms, which, like an orchestra, must be synchronized, otherwise we will not be able to move forward, and

45

we will hear noises instead of music.

How can we make decisions in the best possible way? Being objective, accurate, leaving aside value judgments and subjective data. There is nothing more efficient than accurate data. People say it's hard to do this or that activity, and 80% of the time it's easier than you think.

Dare to err

Reaching high has a price: you must try everything; many actions will go outside the arc. Not being afraid to err is perhaps grandiose, fear is something wise, it matters to us, and it affects us. But I think knowing how to live and coexist with the fear of making mistakes is the key. Live fully, know how to impose yourself, don't say yes to everything and don't fear rejection.

I think that contrary to what common sense says that risk losing is important, I think.... and I share with you..., *risking not to win* should be the flame that must be faced.

Why try it? I am going to give you three fundamental reasons to encourage you to try it, the first has to do precisely with that, so as not to fear

46

making a mistake if you don't try. Great athletes always get angry at those who don't try... nobody gets angry with someone who at least gave it a shot. The second has to do with not letting an opportunity pass by. In this sense, we all know someone who goes through life regretting not having tried something when the opportunity presented itself and not doing it at that moment deprived them of that potential result that could have changed their life forever. The third has to do with the awareness that we generate about ourselves for not having encouraged ourselves to try, which creates a negative and limiting perception about our own Self and self-esteem, which impacts confidence in our abilities to face future challenges.

Trying is the flame, and how do we light that flame? With determination. We can all turn it on, there are no limits, there are no glass ceilings when trying.

Trying is **Doing** the effort and taking the necessary steps to do something or achieve a certain objective or goal, without being absolutely certain of achieving it.

We return to certainty; I share with you that trying without certainty produces at least more certainty than not trying.

I remember when I built and implemented the company's sustainable media business strategy. It was a project that I developed little by little, that I designed with the collaboration of great specialists in the subject who believed in my idea and that I managed to complete thanks to the contribution of many: from employees, volunteers to directors, talents and organizations among others. And something happened that surprised me terribly. We were in the Auditorium of the Malba Museum, on the occasion of the presentation of our first annual sustainability report and the strategic matrix of the sustainable media business. At the moment in which the CEO of the company, until then my boss, Alejandro Harrison, refers in his speech to everything we had achieved as a company in terms of sustainability, what we had managed to develop and how he positioned us in advance with a sustainable media strategy; to my pride and surprise, he in turn highlights that we had achieved the achievement as an organization thanks to my conviction and certainty, and admitting that he

48

himself disbelieved at first when listening to my ideas, but that he let it move forward for two reasons: the first one because I did not ask for a large budget, and second, it was a way to reward the fact that I fulfilled all my responsibilities and exceeded goals and expectations the vast majority of the time.

2. SELL

I don't feel good saying this, but I honestly believe that women in general don't worry about learning how to sell, we don't know how to sell, we don't know how to sell ourselves and believe me, it's super necessary!

Of course, there are many women who are successful at selling, I worked with great salespeople in some sales teams, but they learned the "secret" of selling and I can tell you that they are a minority.

Selling is solving a problem through a product or service. First, we listen to the problem, then we solve it.

49

Suppose we want to sell a certain product or service. Through our skills, do we know what problems we can solve? Yes, yes, they are understandable, but is it difficult for them to find buyers? So, I wonder, are they asking themselves the right questions? Because if I want to sell a certain product to someone who doesn't need it, I won't be able to do it.

If we know that the formula for selling is to find someone who has the problem and solve it, how do we get closer to that person? In the same way we connect to people, through relationships. We will not be able to form a sports team if we do not know players who want to play and with whom we can share those experiences. Selling is the same.

There are dozens of ways to sell, let's remember when we have bought something with happiness... surely the seller took us for a spin with that car, or showed in detail the benefits of a product for the home, or with incredible ability showed it to an economic group that by acquiring a certain company they were going to increase the general profits of the group.

There are three keys to selling:

1. First look at the problem we solve.

2. Second, develop relationships based on accurate information.

3. And third, do not get discouraged in the face of uninteresting responses. Perhaps we are wanting to call a person at an inopportune time.

These 3 keys work, just as a boat navigates on water, in calm and opportune situations. No one wants to interrupt the captain of a sailboat in a storm or when entering or leaving a port, right?

From my experience I can tell you that working in large organizations, you have to do what we call internal sales, where you are the one who solves the problems and that is the reason why they will give you all the support you require.

In this sale of your work for growth, there are three other keys:

1. Listen to your leader, both what they say and what they do not say, but communicate with their body language, and allows you to

understand the urgency, the pressure they have, the problem to be solved and above all "their need" and from where the request is made.

2. Have a positive attitude that generates containment, that calms, that predisposes the other person to clearly transmit their needs and expectations, that they perceive that you are there to resolve the situation, and that there is no doubt that you will be able to do it within the given period.

3. Identify through 2 or 3 questions, never an interrogation, all the data that will allow you to complete the assignment: when it is expected, the required approach and the expectations you have about the result.

Throughout my career, I have noticed that one of the characteristics that allowed me to grow in organizations was being able to deliver the assigned or required work, meeting not only the dates, but also exceeding the expectations regarding the content or result to be achieved. Possibly it is because, although I always had the ability to perceive the needs of others, continuous exercise sharpened this capacity and allowed me to provide solutions that met or exceeded what was expected.

In a corporation, managers always expect solutions to their problems and a job that meets their needs generates prestige in those who do it, so from then on, your possibilities of selling "you" have no limits.

---

3. NEGOTIATE

Negotiating is learned, not so much in theory, but in practice.

Leading a good negotiation involves a lot of prior work of research and analysis, the task is done beforehand. And what does this preparation in the smallest detail consist of? Identifying win-win scenarios seems relatively simple, however it requires several factors:

1. Absolute empathy for the person with whom we negotiate: what are their needs? I do it through deep active listening, from verbal to gestural and physical. This way I understand their expectations.

2. Design of possible scenarios almost like in the

perinola spinning top: everyone loses, everyone wins, only one wins. Additionally, the analysis of pros and cons of each one. The way to do this is by imagining stories with different possible endings. This way I will be prepared for each situation that arises in the negotiation process.

3. Investigation of facts that support my point of view. I have absolute clarity about my situation. I have elements that reliably support me.

4. Know what I am willing to lose and what I should gain. I evaluate each scenario qualitatively and quantitatively. I understand where I stand, what I'm willing to lose and what I can't.

5. Having control over myself is the best way to have control of the situation, because we will never have control over others. Calmness and a clear mind allow me to act slowly and have time to think about each of my words.

A negotiation consists of adding options on one side and comparing with the added options on the other. I remember a friend who, during her

54

divorce, fought over the valuation of an asset instead of considering the outlay of expenses that that asset caused and the true usufruct that it gave her.

We functioned in the same way when I was in charge of mentoring a great woman and very successful executive in America, who asked me to assist her in the negotiations that she carried out on many occasions, given the security that my solid analysis of the different scenarios that could be presented, which perfectly complemented her sanguine negotiation style. In fact, she looked at me with perplexity when I was writing clauses on a computer in the hotel lobby, or when I was doing calculations in the perfect application that we have so that we never feel alone: spreadsheets.

Being clear about what we want to achieve and doing it transparently allows us to act stripped of subjectivity, vested interests, egos and unnecessary ambitions.

In negotiations, two roles are taken: defense and attack, the art is moving in both positions, because if you stand on the side of the attack, the other will end up losing and it will be an unfair negotiation and if at all times you become defensive, you will not be able to present what you have to propose, because you will be focused on constantly avoiding arguments.

Try to remember a negotiation that did not end as you expected, and you will be able to identify that an unforeseen event arose, you were taken by surprise and what you had to give up was not in your plans.

I conclude that a good negotiation is the result of excellent preparation.

4. FINANCE

That numbers are difficult is a great myth that must be debunked. Like all knowledge, it requires dedication and time, without value judgments. Luckily, and unlike most activities in life, in finances $2 + 2 = 4$ without surprises or shocks.

Here I want to bring a personal experience where I have had to mentor a woman, one of the most successful women in Latin America, in the world of entertainment, brilliant in every way, but who had absolutely no knowledge about managing

56

finances.

At this point, and to make you smile I will only ask you 2 questions that are worth learning, first, what is the difference between a simple interest rate and a compound interest rate? And the second one, what do you like more, a one-time ambitious contract, or a not so large periodic contract? You have to be accurate, whatever adds more, this is mathematics.

The first answer is for you to compare alone.

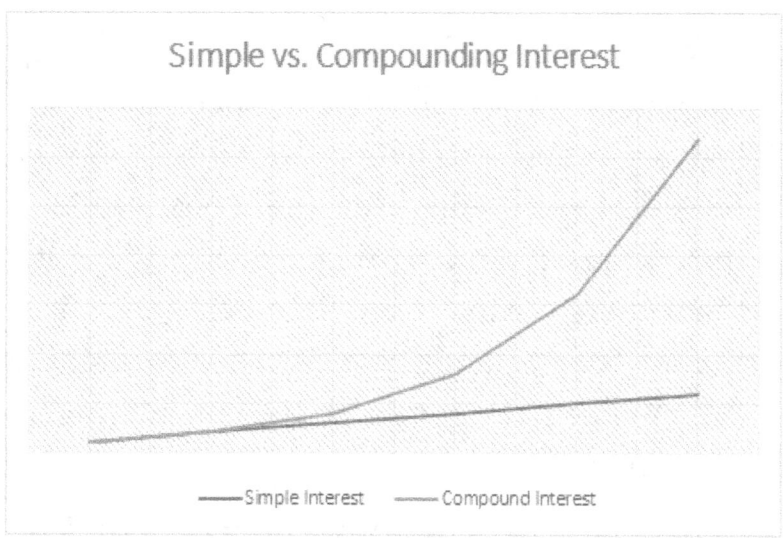

The second answer is easier

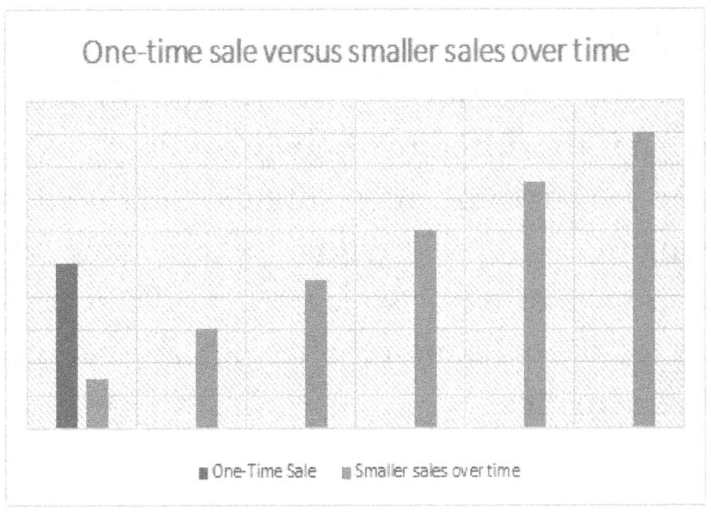

My mentee, who was and is an exceptional woman, always delegated finances to others. She had been taught to live in the present, but without considering potential future income, which meant that, when it came to finances, she did not realize that others earned more than her, and that she did not do well when it came to negotiating. She sold the intellectual rights without considering scalable agreements.

Sorry if I go into this in depth, but I want to dedicate this section to Oliver Hart and Bengt Holmström, 2016 Nobel Prize in Economics for their contribution to contract theory.

In his theory of contracts, he explains why insurance companies never pay the full amount of a claim, and why parties that work for a common good that is scalable over time produce better results. Thinking about clauses in the future tense opens up potential correction negotiations, but establishing limits closes them.

Issues such as conflicts of interest, where one party cannot benefit from the results of another, helped public organizations obtain analysis tools on the convenience of one alternative over another.

In finance, a figure appeared that would have been impossible to think of years ago, which is the analysis of multiple variable scenarios. I know a financial analyst who spent 3 or 4 days on his computer producing scenario calculations to get to a meeting and modify a price that no one had set that would produce millions of profits after several years.

Without pretending to be economists, knowing about finances is having the possibility of being able to interact in the business world, to understand the variables, to lose the fear of terms such as: profits, profitability, margin, financial risk, accrual, marginal percent, return on investment, among others, and be familiar with them. Learn them like any other concept.

Finance is the axis on which all organizations move, public, private and even non-profit ones. It is our responsibility not only to know them but to master them and the collateral benefit is the dialogue that we will be able to establish with businessmen and women.

Understanding finances is required regardless of the origin of your profession. If you are independent, knowing them will allow you to grow economically, know how to invest or disinvest, if you are an employee it will help you know how to generate value in the business and industry you work in and you will be recognized for it and if you are an entrepreneur, becoming the owner of your finances will guarantee taking care of your income and expenses like no one else could.

5. NETWORKS / LINKS

Let's be clear, you can never grow alone. In this regard, I remember a lunch with another executive, who wanted to show me that there are professional sports that are individual, to which I asked him very calmly, what if I show you that all sports are team sports? If I win the debate, you invite the bill for the meal, deal? All sure of himself, he said yes and answered: "Tennis, individual, not couples' tournaments." Knowing I had already won the bet, I took a few seconds to respond, "dear, in that sport as in any other, there is a nutritionist, a physical trainer, a coach, and dozens of people who accompany the athlete in his growth, without them he cannot grow". Needless to say, I enjoyed that lunch paid for by the counterparty :).

Networks are about understanding that nothing can be done alone, entrepreneurs depend on clients, but also on suppliers; employees must learn leadership to help their leaders lead them; Work teams learn from each other and from other teams, families, friends, study centers, students, contacts, everything becomes a network that completely supports people's growth.

Healthy relationships, not toxic and dependent, but those based on personal and professional respect, with the correct self-esteem, without selfishness or greed, are the fuel of ambition, which allows it to be contagious, healthy and even fun.

Networking consists of nothing more nor less than forming a network of contacts that at some point help us get a new professional opportunity or perhaps attract clients for our business.

The network of contacts that we generate and later also take care of, will give us endless possibilities in the work, commercial or business world.

Now, this function is more naturally associated with men, and in general women stay behind the desk more pushing the pencil, am I wrong? Well, let me tell you, what may seem like an impossible mission is not, any of us can and in fact has several contacts that you haven't even noticed! Because don't forget that, just as any relationship men establish and immediately add to their network, such as friends from the club, from the neighborhood, from school, we also know women from the gym, moms from school, from the hairdresser, the building, from university, our job, etc., etc., etc. and as I explain below, you will see how we can all do *Networking*.

First of all, be clear about the goal. It is vital that before building a network and doing *networking*, we know what the goal will be, what we are pursuing, since the options are diverse, such as having more clients, generating new business, changing our profession, finding a better position or simply having a greater number of professional contacts with whom to share the experience.

Secondly, it is not about accumulating many contacts due to volume but rather, getting contacts that are truly complementary, useful and offer possibilities.

Thirdly, never overlook people you already know or who your friends know, they can be a very interesting option to link you to a professional area. If they are already contacts that you have created during your training or previous job, they may be useful since they are part of the same professional area that you are focused on.

63

Fourthly, and perhaps the most complicated point, is how to generate contact once you have your network identified. Well, today's social networks give you a great opportunity for that. You can also contact them via email, if you managed to obtain that information or they provided it to you in person, when you attended conferences, events, forums or conventions.

Of course, LinkedIn is a separate chapter in itself. Keep in mind that most businessmen and professionals have a profile on this network, and you are a maximum of 7 clicks away from connecting with anyone you want, this makes it a great opportunity to expand your contacts. You will know the contacts of your contacts and in turn the contacts they have.

Fifthly, do not forget that it is a path in both directions, so you must offer something of interest to the potential contact that you want to incorporate into your network. You can help them with a task, provide some advice, participate in their projects or businesses, or allow them access to those who are already your contacts.

Sixth and lastly, I recommend that you maintain

64

regular communication with your contacts, it does not have to be weekly with everyone, any method can be useful, but the important thing is that you do not limit yourself to adding them to your list and abandoning them until some topic of interest links you to them, you must always keep the interest alive.

6. TECHNOLOGY

I will add a sixth enabler for growth, and a very important one! But first I want to explain how this enabler was incorporated.

When I published my book for my 51st birthday in June 2020, my country and the world had been in several months of quarantine and unthinkable challenges for humanity. A single company with hundreds of employees from one month to the next had to begin managing its entire operation remotely with employees at home, confined due to the global health risk of COVID. Without technology, would we have been able to face it? From one day to the next, even family birthdays are celebrated using video teleconferences. Hasn't the world changed since the appearance of the iPhone in 2007, or the iPad a while later? Isn't it a challenge to even publish a book? Is it thanks to technology that great global ventures such as UBER, Airbnb, Mercado Libre, Glovo, Rappi, Zoom, and thousands more appeared and made our lives easier and more efficient? Is it a coincidence that Amazon and Apple are the first companies in history to surpass a trillion-dollar valuation in 2019? And Mercado Libre with a valuation of more than $50 billion due to the development of its ecommerce and Fintech technology such as Mercado Pago?

Can you run a business without using Microsoft Excel? Imagine the best data analysts in the world; They are not just the best because of the content alone, but because they use MS Excel better than anyone else. Why? Well, they are experts in macros, yes, they make programs in minutes in a programming language, and they make spreadsheets work magic. With macros I have seen payrolls generate receipts to employees and send emails with attached files in PDF format, and at the same time connect via IP to the bank and make the transfers. If only 10% of 1,000 entrepreneurs use Excel, that is, 100, imagine those who use macros, only another 10% of them, perhaps 10 out of every 1,000 users. But this next question is to make you smile, do you know someone who makes macros in Excel and connects them with macros in Microsoft Word to verify term clouds and analyze grammatical syntax? It is clear that these people can do the work of dozens of analysts for months, alone and in just a few weeks. I have seen it, analysts who calculate thousands of financial scenarios for a company using models. This way it is easier and safer to grow.

It seems like science fiction, but I want to go to a real example of a multinational, in this case I am using the example of a colleague because I found it magnificent due to its simplicity.

Personal story: Excel in Action

In one of the world's leading multinationals, with more than 300,000 employees, there was a CxO in London who was very concerned about some variables that the shareholder committee had asked him to analyze. He had a great challenge, to study this data, he depended on many people. In Europe, more than 90 billing systems were used, most of them in Oracle, and in Asia more than 30 in SAP. There was no way to analyze this data. Requesting a report could take weeks of validations until authorizations were generated to modify the databases.

On a trip to New York, he met that analyst who I mentioned before that not only did macros in Excel but even did them in Word. As light as possible, he told this executive, "Don't worry, we will solve it in 2 days. Don't ask for any modifications to the systems, no one will understand anything, and it will take months. Do you know why they won't understand it? Well, the analysis has not yet been created in your mind, and you cannot ask people to do what anyone, not you, not the shareholder committee asked you to do." With a restless but curious voice, the CxO asked, "... but... How can we do it?" The answer was not long in coming, it came from knowledge of the technology, "It's easy, we ask for the reports they have, in the text or pdf format that they can, don't worry, with a couple of hours I transform them into text, I change the format in Word, I convert the line changes into tabs to create columns in Excel, and then we import it into Excel and make dynamic tables to calculate models that help you understand results in minutes."

Without going into detail, I tell you that they did have problems with the limits of Excel, which only supports one million rows. Then they made columns that did not exceed this limitation, one next to the other, and began to analyze them in combination, in a 64-bit operating system, seeking to work with statistical models, that is, using only 7% of the data at the time at random, to have a margin of error of less than 0.5%. They combined them in minutes. The program? It was no more than 5 pages.

Let's understand the challenge, an executive made decisions using Excel, being able to share those spreadsheets with other executives, in days, not in weeks or months. Nobody needed passwords or access to complicated systems, they just needed the most fabulous tool that people should know: spreadsheets. And macros, of course!

Do you want more everyday examples? Who doesn't know someone who complains about the speed of their computer or that their phone is slower? Well, I tell you, there are programs that clean up what we don't use, making them faster.

Learning about technology is perhaps one of the most important challenges for people who have not developed these skills. It is not necessary to study many details, but a little more than what we know, especially the Office platforms of the main references in the world, Microsoft, Apple, Google, and many more.

It will make us faster. What others do in days, we will do in hours; What many people stay until midnight and on weekends working on, we can finish early and go pick up our children from school to do their homework with them.

The dimensions of technological growth

I am convinced that technology is a great enabler. It may happen that your *background* is *techie* or *geek* but if your training is in other areas, as is my case, who comes from the world of numbers, it is a necessity to incorporate technological knowledge and constantly update yourself.

Knowing, and if possible, mastering technological aspects opens up infinite possibilities. They are developed from five areas:

70

1. **Autonomy:** Knowing technological tools allows you to be totally independent when doing your work, but also when you have to protect it (make a backup for example, and then find it, and then restore it!). You don't need anyone to manage your passwords, you know what to do when your computer does not respond or when it is necessary to update the software on your devices, to name a few. It is not just about knowing how to do it, but understanding what is happening to handle the tools with complete confidence or to discover problems and not act by reading instructions.

   It's the weekend, you need to do a task that involves technological aspects, you can do it without waiting for Monday to go to someone to guide you.

2. **Speed:** We have to accept it, technology consumes time, and a lot of it, especially if we do not master it, it is highly likely that we will invest double or triple our time in doing something that is not the focus of our work. Knowing how to standardize a document prevents us from having to make changes manually and we can concentrate on the

content, freeing ourselves from the format. Not wasting time in the format gives speed, and also gives security.

3. **Positioning:** In your professional career, you will have many opportunities where you are offered new roles, they will make you grow, and you will have people in charge. Knowing the tools that we use daily allows you to better position yourself in leadership roles because teams need their leaders to also know how to guide them on technology issues or at least understand the tools available on the market and what value each one brings to business.

Being able to organize a meeting in minutes or know the alternative solutions for virtual meetings, the pros and cons of each one; share documentation and files on platforms; manage projects in SharePoint or Trello, share a whiteboard to work on a project with your team or colleagues through a collaborative tool like MURAL, says something about you. What you convey is that you took time to learn technological solutions, that you are interested in being up to date, that age is not an impediment, and that even though the world of technology continues to evolve, you decided to advance at the same pace.

Mastering Excel produces magic, remember that.

Your team, and those around you, understand that if you confidently handle technology, how much more mastery you will have of the issues for which you have responsibility; how much more can teams feel accompanied by someone who is not at a disadvantage regarding an issue that is essential to them. Mainly technology, much more in a person who not only has knowledge and confidence.

4. **Business Value:** Today we can say that learning about the solutions offered by the market marks a new era when it comes to decision making. Having the possibility of doing data analysis in a structured way to predict or analyze the behavior of employees, customers, channels, market, products, etc. It is radically different from estimating some possibilities with information we obtain from mere research.

Regardless of the business or industry you are in, when you know what the different tools

73

provide, it allows you to bring a value proposition to the strategic table, as Steve Jobs said under the motto: "*connecting the dots*". The moment you are presented with a problem or need, that tool that you learned about or was told about, and you know could cover the needs presented, will resonate in your head. There are countless examples such as zoom for virtual collaborative work, or analytics to predict or simulate situations for decision making, and countless B2B, B2C, E2E (employee to employee) connectivity tools.

Shall I tell you a trick? Placing a nice logo on your emails or on your sites and communications connected to the Google Analytics service means that you not only know if they read the email or not, but you will also be able to analyze incredible dimensions by locations, data networks, devices, etc.

5. **Inclusion:** knowing aspects of technology allows you to include more people in your area, by promoting multidisciplinary teams, you will be able to expand your network with those who master the technology. I've met executives who work with writers who in turn work with geeks

and really make magic in their reports.

Other people will be able to call you because you will have a common point that is increasingly an axis for growth. Understanding technology, without having to be an expert, is the first step to continue learning and adopting different range of tools.

I challenge you to study your tools a little more, to stop saying "it's difficult", "I can't", "I don't know", "I don't understand", "I don't have time", and every day let yourself be approached by the curiosity and seek to learn a little more. Perhaps the first change they should make is to use technology more, every time they want to do something ask on the internet, perhaps there is a three-minute video on YouTube that will save them hours of work, let's not be stupid, to grow you need to use all the resources and make them available to us.

Do we use Google search well? They know that if they put the words they are looking for with a "+" in front and others with a "-" in front, Google will look for information that DOES have some words and does NOT have others. It is basic, but I know that few use it, let's start little by little, every day we advance and incorporate resources of a few millimeters, in a year it will be meters and over time the ability to manage this area will give us a differential, which is very satisfactory and valued.

SECOND PART

SKILLS

Only with the heart can one see correctly.
The essential is invisible to the eyes.
Antoine de Saint-Exupéry.

CORE SKILLS

"If passion, if madness did not ever pass through souls... What would life be worth?"
-Jacinto Benavente-

For me, this is the fundamental ingredient, doing what we choose every day with passion, it's that, I don't know to describe it, that flame that lights up and that gives us strength when everyone is already tired, that illuminates us with an idea when everyone has already lowered their arms, which allows us to see things clearly when everyone sees it dark or cannot see it at all. But also, it is that quality that allows us not to feel the fatigue of the rest, that does not stress us as much as it should if we do not see ourselves self-motivated by our *cuore*, for the passion of doing what we dream of, what we like, what makes the hours fly and we do not

79

notice that we are still in the company, in your venture, in a project, whatever it is that you are passionate about.

1. CORE

Working with the core of your body, your heart, for me is making the impossible possible and what allows you to understand and demonstrate that there are no limits, except those that your mind sets for yourself.

But when I mention passion, what exactly do I mean? What does it mean in real life?

The heart is related to passion as an intense feeling, it involves desire, enthusiasm for something, it can be an activity, a cause, a person, anything we can imagine.

It is important to clarify that dedicating yourself to your passion does not guarantee enjoyment 100% of the time, since following a passion also requires sacrifices and effort, and at times suffering may even be present.

When you find your passion, you are willing to dedicate yourself, even when doing so often requires demanding yourself and giving beyond your strength and on the other hand, knowing how to say no, even if it costs you; Otherwise, when this does not happen, it is a hobby.

Personal story: When you are passionate about what you do

And here I go with my story, one of the many that I treasure, where I show an example in which passion is revealed.

It turns out that it's Friday, some of my friends invite me to have a drink and update us on our lives.

Here I open a parenthesis to say that one of the things that I am grateful for in life are the friends that I have, I have friends from my different stages of life and the diversity of activities that I did and do so intensely during these first 50 years of life. I have my first best friend Cecilia, my daughter's godmother, whom I caressed from her mother's belly (my godmother of the heart) and to whom I always tell that she was born with a best friend under her arm. But also, I have my friends from school, from college, from sports, from postgraduate studies, from jobs, from projects, from the gym, from the mothers of my daughter's

82

friends, from colleagues, from former bosses and from different generations. I have friends who are 20, 30, 40, 50, 60, 70 and 80 years old, and with each of them, the experiences that I shared and still share were and are different, but they are all rich, fun, wise, exciting, comforting, important and so I can continue with several more qualities of those wonderful relationships, but before going on about them, let's return to the anecdote.

It's 7 pm. approximately, I receive a message from them, from my friends in their thirties, and I, obviously, in my office working on the desk issues that are attended to after the whirlwind of meetings and *calls* of the day, tasks such as reading contracts, signing payments, reviewing reports, which require concentration and during the course of a work day it is difficult to find the space, since it is occupied with our teams, colleagues and social commitments. Candelaria, my daughter, was at one of her friends' houses for a sleepover, and I had no plans, but even so I didn't commit to my friends' invitation, although when they insisted, I told them to let me know when they were on their way since the idea was to go to a bar in Palermo Soho, a few blocks from the company. I, without imagining it, immerse myself passionately in the project that I was reviewing and adjusting, and when I look at the clock, from the sound that my stomach emits due to the languor that I felt at that time, I see that it was 11 p.m. and that I had received a message from my friends a few minutes before, letting me know as we agreed, that they were on their way to the Palermitano meeting. I, tired, begin to gather things to go home and put everything in my *carry-on* where I carried the notebook, documents, chargers, books and everything that allowed me to stay connected during the weekend, if I wanted.

I go towards the garage, which at that time was half a block from the building, and I come across them! They are divine, well-groomed and smiling! Ready to spend a great night of adventure. I was dressed in a corporate suit, without makeup, my hair was messy, and my eyes were tired. That's when we collided, literally, I look up because the laughter sounded familiar and they said to me, let's go! To which I respond that in addition to feeling tired, I wanted to avoid embarrassing them, since although the idea was to catch up while we had a few drinks, there is always the possibility of meeting people and honestly with my appearance at that moment, the best idea was to leave my meeting with them for another day, to which after a joint laugh, they look at me, smile knowingly with me and agree with my decision, we said goodbye with a hug...

I love meetings with friends, as much as I loved that time where I reviewed and adjusted the project I was analyzing, that is feeling passionate about what we do, that feeling of losing track of time by being immersed in doing what you are passionate about.

Something about passion and success...

Passion is a fundamental ingredient that helps you achieve your success. Why? Well, to achieve excellence, a theory by Malcolm Gladwell[2] explains, along with some skills and talents, around 10,000 hours of investment in the field are required. That is why passion is considered essential, since you would not be willing to invest 10,000 hours in something that you are not passionate about.

But the fact that passion is present is not enough

---

[2] Libro Outliers – Malcom Gladwell

to be successful. Passion gives you the strength and drive to move forward to conquer what you want, but without skills, energy alone cannot achieve it, at most what it does is give you the engine that allows you to learn certain skills that you may be lacking, but there must be a fundamental surrender on your part.

Roger Federer / Rick Allen

It is always easier to show the passions in an athlete or an artist than in an executive, which is why it is easier for us to think of Roger Federer, the first Swiss to win a *Grand Slam*, who says that his career changed in 2003 when he decided to set in his head that he could achieve it and in July of that year he became the winner of Wimbledon. I also remember the case of Rick Allen, famous drummer of the band Def Leppard, who shortly after forming the band, had his left arm amputated because of an accident in which his limb was injured. And although he immediately entered a depressive pit, he returned to activity, thanks to the support of his colleague Joe Elliot and a group of

86

engineers who specially conditioned the battery so that it could be handled with one hand. With great dedication and sacrifice, Rick overcomes adversity due to the passion he generated from making music and playing that instrument.

But I assure you that the passion of Roger or Rick is also felt by us women who develop our passions in other areas, artistic, sports, cultural and also professional and business.

Frida Kahlo

But since it is about women, we have a list of excellent references and sources of inspiration to work on ourselves and our development. In this chapter, honoring its theme, I want to mention one among many other passionate women who left their mark, such as Frida Kahlo, who managed to transcend through her innovative works of art and who is currently remembered as one of the most famous artists of the 20th century. True to her passions, she sought to do things differently and respond to them, from painting to more personal issues in her life such as her sexual orientation and challenging stereotypes.

Now, to close the chapter, I want to leave you some inspiring questions that encourage you, mobilize you and invite you to energize doing!

Questions for your own reflection

1. *Do you feel passionate about what you do?*

2. *Do you feel like you have an infinite source of energy when you work on the project you've been looking forward to?*

3. *Do you feel like you are not stressed, even if you sleep 4 hours or work against the clock on weekends trying to exceed your goals?*

4. *Do you feel like you are like a fish in water?*

5. *Do you feel like you wake up and after a good shower you run the world around you?*

6. *Do you feel that you are a fundamental part of the machine?*

7. *Do you feel that with your actions you change a small part of the world?*

If you are not feeling any of this, then I invite you to explore these other questions:

1. *What things make you feel fulfilled?*

2. *What area do you vibrate in? Do you like art? Do you*

like interacting with people? Are you good at planning? Do you find solutions where others don't? Do you have the ability to express yourself? Do numbers seem magical to you? Do you enjoy organizing things?

3. *Are you curious? Do you accept risks? How do you get along with new things?*

Do you have a dream that you always put off because it seemed too crazy or impossible?

2. CHARISMA

"Charisma is a spark in people that money cannot buy. It is an invisible energy with visible effects."
Marianne Williamson.

"People who love life have charisma because they fill the room with positive energy."
John C. Maxwell.

When we refer to charisma, we understand its origin in a Greek word that means "to please", from there the term charisma is derived, referring to the capacity of people to attract and captivate others. Charisma is something innate and is part of the human being's personality. Those who possess personal charisma exhibit values and beliefs that attract their followers and are at the same time imitated by them. Words like competence, integrity, ethics, passion, strength, and confidence are tied to the concept of charisma.

It is identified as a capacity associated with success, based on the conception that a charismatic person does well in life. For this reason, many claim that by helping a person strengthen their self-esteem, their abilities as a speaker and their appearance, we are helping them become charismatic.

The doctrine held by the sociologist Max Weber, considers that charisma allows the people to have some form of power, since individuals notice an extraordinary personality in the charismatic leader and for that reason, they allow themselves to be led by him. The charismatic leader is not always positive to the environment, in fact this type of leadership was the one that enabled Adolf Hitler, for example, to construct and use his leadership and power in a destructive manner that lacked total rationality.

The vast majority of leaders have a special charisma, which largely outweighs their professional or intellectual merits; And because of that ability, they have the power to group their followers and make them believe in their words and comply with their requests and adhere to their purposes.

We will surely agree that a charismatic leader is someone who connects well with others, brings out the best in each person, and above all knows how to conduct himself and adapt to different contexts. They are confident, spontaneous and convey confidence and optimism. They carry a kind of magnetism that inspires others to follow them. For this reason, experts conclude that charisma is one of the most powerful forms of leadership, as identified in personalities such as Gandhi, Hitler, Roosevelt, Napoleon, Kennedy and Barak Obama among others.

Characteristics of a charismatic leader

They have a great capacity for conviction. They are able to modify the scale of values, beliefs and attitudes of their followers. They are excellent motivators, capable of taking risks, create admiration and have a vision for the future.

It is also important to understand that it is not just about being charismatic, but about behaving as such. Among the most common characteristics of these leaders, the ones that I find most assertive are:

Knowing how to listen to and reflect on the ideas of others, with openness, without prejudice and without devaluing them because they do not coincide with yours. This skill is very important since no person with charisma will receive the trust of others if people perceive that their superior ignores their proposals, and only considers their own valid. The charismatic leader is interested in what happens to others.

They inspire and generate confidence, this ability is fundamental and is one of those obtained through experience and acting by example, which is why it requires a period of maturation, a person does not suddenly trust another. Through their actions, they must show the ability to recognize and seek solutions to their own mistakes and make others understand their successes and mistakes. And something fundamental that you should consider is that just as generating credibility and trust requires investing time, it is lost in a single moment, and it's highly unlikely that that leader will be considered as a reference again among his followers.

They pursue excellence, and never settles, which is why the charismatic person, when they perceive an error or injustice in their environment, does not let it pass and starts the necessary process to solve

94

that problem. Their charismatic imprint leads to action, and this leads to generating change.

They are visionary, so beyond having good ideas, being skilled in certain fields or being very productive, the charismatic leader is capable of developing a project that distinguishes them since they can anticipate what is to come, when the rest looks surprised and may even question their ideas due to lack of clarity and lack of future vision that makes it impossible for them to see beyond what is normally planned or set out in standards.

They take risks and sacrifices, by virtue of the vision of the goal they seek to achieve. The charismatic person leads by example, therefore, acts in line with the ideas they propose. You cannot ask others for something that you are not willing to give.

They are creative. This is how ingenuity and the ability to separate and even abandon predetermined conceptions distinguish a charismatic person from another who is simply competent. Their aspirations are different from those of the rest of the mortals (conformists), who require a series of diverse skills that help them lead projects. The concept spread by the genius Albert Einstein is already well known, which states that if you want different results, you must follow different methods.

They do not criticize others, even if others have made mistakes. Whispering behind your colleagues' backs only leads to their loss of trust. Deep down, the most charismatic people are charismatic because they appear human, although it may sound paradoxical: they recognize that anyone can make a mistake, even if they know how to hide it well, and they remember that the important thing is to learn from it and not repeat it.

They talk about "we", not "I". Egocentrism is not exactly a common quality among charismatic people; but involving others in the project that one has started is. What is important is the common goal and that each person adopts the role that the company needs, not the personal achievement of the leader.

And here is my story, related to this very special and particular ability that is charisma.

Personal story: Achieving restructuring with the support of the entire team

The media industry, since 1995 onwards, has been going through a contraction in business volumes and results, largely a product of the increase in labor costs due to the high tax pressure on labor. As well as the increase in costs generated from the greater burdens and union demands that companies have been compensating through the balance between the increase in productivity levels and the decrease in staffing. Additionally, movement in the media industry is frequent and constant, so mergers and acquisitions are always the order of the day and, as you already know, they are processes that greatly affect people and work teams.

I led three major restructurings during my tenure as SVP of Human Resources Regional, as well as in my role as Country Manager based in Argentina for Latin America for a renowned media company.

They represented a very important objective for the company, basically for three fundamental reasons, the first, because the labor cost line was the item with the greatest participation in the company's total costs. Secondly, the business depended on labor, which generated a great contingency due to the dependence on human resources at different points in the process, both in the insertion of the material and in the uploading of the signal to the satellite. And thirdly, because of the collateral damage that the brand could receive, given the potential impact in the event that the process achieved a negative impact in the media.

With all this, I prepared to lead these restructuring projects, at different times, all of them important and of great impact, but I am going to stop at the last one, as it was also the process that additionally promoted my departure from the corporation.

It all started around mid-2013 when the analysis requested by the new shareholders showed a terrible equation in relation to the continuity of the business based in Argentina, since from here we produced, marketed and carried out the complete operation for Latin America.

This result led to the decision to reduce the operation in Buenos Aires to a minimum, 70 vs. 350 employees at that time, and to generate different production centers and commercial offices in countries in the region with a better-quality ratio of professionals, labor costs, tax pressure and legal security.

By then I had two hats, SVP HR Regional and Country Manager Southern Cone, so, once the decision was made, they offered me the HR position based in Miami, considering that the Country Manager position was disappearing from the organization chart.

I will leave the analysis and decision of my transfer for another chapter of this book, but where I want to focus on is the management and leadership of this project, which I agreed to lead and which required detailed planning that contemplated several aspects, from reviewing plans exit, union negotiations, crisis committee, contingency plans, work environment management, change management, *startup* of new territories and *downsizing* of Argentina, definition of GANTT, project costing and negotiation of funds and items.

One Sunday afternoon at my desk, I sit in front of the finished plan, with a cup of hot tea, feeling the vertigo that I anticipated the next day. I had to start involving the entire team, since only 3 of them had accompanied me up to that point, and it is at that precise moment that I decide that it will be charisma and attributes that it brings, that were going to allow me to navigate in those turbulent waters.

What I tell you now did not appear in my mind at that moment with the conceptual clarity that I have when writing this book, instead, I simply began to think about how I was going to handle each part and the project as a whole. For example, I knew that the best thing was to communicate to my direct reports in a transparent way what the project was about and listen to them, receive their ideas, their criticism and, above all, their emotions, to be able to improve things where we had room to do so, adjust the points that could be perfected and support and accompany the anxieties, feelings of uncertainty, vertigo, fear and even anguish that naturally occur in these cases. I also planned to always be very close to them and their teams, always communicating my shared vision with the new shareholders in relation to the opportunity for business growth. I took care of providing support

100

and inspiring them to find new dreams, seek new horizons, whether occupying different roles in the company once it was reorganized, or challenging themselves to develop other roles outside the company, I pushed them to leave the placid comfort zone, where I was sure that everyone could give more than what they had displayed up to that moment.

Everything had to be perfect and there were many variables, all with a high degree of complexity, which led me to invite them to design a dashboard that would allow us to monitor, calibrate and adjust the different actions of the project.

Of course, it was about taking a risk, and within the project, many more emerged periodically, but from the front I extended my hand to them so that they felt supported, followed me and could see that there was more light in front of us than behind what we were leaving and rebuilding.

I sought to infect and invite my team to pursue excellence in every step, see how we could improve, how to perfect each thing that was planned, how we were building more and better together.

We checked the pulse of the company all the time, I spent hours and hours talking to people, always transparently, explaining that the current conditions, in which the company's business was developed, were not viable to sustain itself in the future. I also taught them the beneficial possibilities that the company offered for their exit, the way in which I could accompany them, recommending their skills, knowledge and experience to develop in other companies. It was a reality from which they did not get out due to poor performance, on the contrary, they were being expelled by an organization that had no way of continuing to provide employment opportunities, but many of them had some project, or abandoned dream, or had a family member or friend with a certain challenge where they could contribute, in short, hundreds of opportunities that they only had to help them visualize, develop, accompanying them, listening to them, containing them and allowing them to lead the way.

Also, I monitored the general climate and prepared everything for the change that was coming, so that the employees who remained in the

102

structure could make the new business model their own and take ownership of the challenges, functioning in a way that guaranteed giving their best, as until now, and even take some opportunity to develop in an alternative area or position that would provide them with growth in their careers.

But not to be confused, these qualities inherent to charisma were absolutely necessary but not sufficient, which is why they did not stop being combined and assembled all the time with the search for the general goal of the company, which with vision, determination, results orientation and excellence, I never lost sight of for a moment.

The project concluded on time, occupying the 24 months of the GANTT, achieving all and even exceeding some objectives established by the shareholders, improving indicators in all areas and contributing value to the company at an international level.

While it is true that many people are innately charismatic, many of the characteristics of charisma that I have mentioned are perfectly possible to develop and put into practice, walking the path and overcoming the various situations that arise in a field of action, allow you to deploy them, make mistakes and improve.

Coco Chanel

Who I want to bring in a special way in this chapter is Coco Chanel, since if there is someone who marked a before and after in the world of fashion, through her charisma, it was Coco. During the First World War she dared and left opulent feminine dresses aside and adapted traditionally masculine garments with a simple and comfortable style. She also developed complementary product lines, such as bags, perfumes, hats and jewelry. She is the only fashion designer to appear on Time magazine's list of the one hundred most influential people of the 20th century.

Questions for your own reflection

1. *How many times have you applied your charisma in situations that allowed you to do better?*

2. *On how many occasions would having handled some situations with charisma have helped you achieve better results?*

3. *How are you in relation to your listening? Do you take into account the ideas and opinions of others?*

4. *And your vision? Are you a risk taker?*

5. *How could you demystify that charisma is exclusive to some people?*

6. *Did you have opportunities, of any kind, work, sports or family, where you motivated others?*

7. *Are you creative? Are you looking for different ways to do things?*

8. *Are you one of the women who has a great critical eye to identify external errors but does not have self-criticism?*

9. *How do you deal with the example? Do you act like you preach and demand from others?*

10.   *Are you up to deploy your imagination and visualize yourself with charisma in any situation you choose? What do you think? What would you leave and what would you change?*

3. CONFIDENCE

"If people like you, they will listen to you, but if they trust you, they will do business with you."
Zig Ziglar

"It is mutual trust, rather than mutual interest, that keeps human groups together."
H. L. Mencken

"It takes 20 years to build a reputation and five minutes to ruin it."
Warren Buffett

Confidence is a skill that I consider extremely important and that I will cover both in terms of having confidence in yourself and trust in others. It is my intention to help you understand its importance and why we should cultivate it more and better.

In sociology and social psychology, it is said that trust is the belief that a person or group will be able and willing to act appropriately in a given situation.

Being honest, noble, honorable and fair in doing

and treating others generates trust. On the other hand, the person who only cares about their own interests, and does everything in order to satisfy them, generates distrust.

Trust will be more or less reinforced depending on actions and values. Trust and credibility are the golden rules by which personal relationships are measured and which also apply to the links between people and brands.

Regarding trust towards third parties and how to generate credibility in others, these being your reports and their extended teams, clients, shareholders, suppliers and many others, I would like to tell you about some actions that make it possible, almost without you realizing them:

Always be honest, even if being honest means some loss for you, it may be that way this time, but I guarantee that it generates incredible long-term bonds, based on one hundred percent credibility.

It is always much better to be honest in advance, recognize mistakes, expose gaps and even show yourself vulnerable, because that situation will define the foundations of what you can and will be able to build, otherwise it not only does not

108

generate trust and credibility, but it completely destroys it.

Personal story: The benefits of doing the right thing

I went through more than one situation with complete honesty, but the strongest and most emblematic one was when I prepared and presented the business report and advised the shareholders on the convenience of not maintaining the operation in Buenos Aires, even if this meant that my position as General Manager that I enjoyed so much would disappear. The reality was that, although I left the position, they gave me the opportunity to go as SVP HR Global to NYC. I left an incredible bond with Josh Sapan and Ed Carrol at AMC Networks, and it also enabled me to open a new chapter with Engineer Hernán Lombardi, who invited me and took on the challenge of transforming the Public Media of Argentina, allowing me to leave a mark in my country, in the industry that I love so much. And it also prepared me much better to begin to outline the path on which today I am traveling more than happy, more than blissful.

Learn to say no

Therefore, never distort reality, get to the point and in a transparent way, commenting on advantages and disadvantages, you will go on the safe path.

Do not promise anything that you cannot fulfill, since sooner or later the cure will be worse than the disease.

Some professionals can't resist saying no to a manager, their boss, a superior, or a client about something. But remember that a "no" in time is better than many yeses when they may not have support to be followed.

Do not accept or offer gifts or bribes, since they are always frowned upon, they leave you at the door of rewarding with a favor that you may not want to be giving and additionally it is unethical from the beginning.

When you do not have a Compliance area or person in charge of Compliance in your company, who is responsible for defining, implementing and communicating these specific rules, which discourage and even prevent bad practices, seek to evaluate them through a pass or fail filter, aimed at extreme caution, since it will always help you.

Be sure of our value

Now regarding personal confidence, let me tell you that self-confidence means being sure of our own worth, ability and power, regardless of the situation we find ourselves in. Someone who is confident then has a strong sense of self-esteem and self-confidence, which translates into expressing serenity, calmness, and self-awareness.

That is why it is very important to develop confidence or security in yourself, since this will lead you to vibrate, feeling confident about yourself and your talent. But beware! Never from a proud and arrogant place, but in a realistic way, which does not mean feeling superiority over others, but rather providing a unique and different contribution, from an inner place that allows you to know that you are capable of doing this or that thing and that calm, peace and tranquility invades you. That allows you to face everything with more temperance, with conviction, and also enables you to convey to others that you are a capable person and that you can contribute.

111

All people, men and women, have felt a lack of confidence or insecurity in oneself at various times in life, this develops a barrier between what we are and what we want to be.

And I have bad news and good news to give you. I'll start with the bad one, a lack of confidence definitely limits the potential you have and becomes an obstacle to achieving your goals. But the good news is that abandoning the feeling of fear and insecurity and gaining confidence is a skill that is learned and developed, which is why I invite you to put it into practice.

The lack of self-confidence is undoubtedly related to fear, since if you don't believe in yourself and you are afraid of not being able to achieve your goal, then you don't even try.

I once heard a representation about this situation that seemed very graphic to me, and I bring it to share it. Imagine yourself on the edge of a bridge, okay? Wanting! Wishing to be on the other side of the bridge! Yeah? But feeling that your feet are almost glued to the place where you are, and that every time you take one of them off to take a step forward, the palpitations accelerate and the cold sweat begins, and they return to the same place where the symptoms are normalizing. Do you get it? Well, the shore where you are is the comfort zone, the shore you want to reach is what you want to achieve, and in the middle of the bridge an imaginary line of fear that prevents you from advancing to the other side, the goal, exists.

Many times, we feel fear, lack of confidence in ourselves, fear of exposure, of what people will say, of failing when I am studying something new, of failing an exam, of failing in a project, of not achieving a dream, of letting someone down. And I could mention a host of everyday and much simpler situations such as a haircut, traveling alone, learning to sing or dance, approaching someone and saying *hello!* And so on I could make a huge list of things…

But I invite you to think, what happens if we try? The feeling of starting is wonderful, it is precisely the energy that allows you to leave the safety zone. And when you move, what you do is expand that area, making our self-confidence increasingly broader.

The reasons why we feel a lack of confidence are basically due to negative thoughts, more than 50% of our thoughts are, in all people, it is not exclusive to women, nor does it only happen to you. Most of the time they are based on negative experiences from the past, but the lack of confidence worsens when you become paralyzed and don't try. I want you to always remember this reflection: <u>It's not failure that's destroying your confidence, not trying again is.</u>

An example that illustrates this situation excellently is the statistic that shows that the baseball players with the greatest records of *home runs* (best plays) also have the highest records of *strikeouts* (worst plays), so it is clearly proven that leaving the comfort zone, crossing the fear zone, takes us to the action zone and from there to the success zone.

But there is another cause that usually fuels insecurity or lack of confidence, and it is pessimistic expectations. In general, developing the expectation that everything will go wrong generates defense mechanisms that allow you not to be disappointed if you fail and get a nice surprise if you succeed.

114

This logic isn't really the best way to deal with insecurity, as research shows that pessimism minimizes your performance. Additionally, it also influences your non-verbal language, since insecurity is not only felt, but also demonstrated; and this non-verbal language has influence where you can least imagine it. This is how different studies have shown that people with triumphant postures have a lower level of stress and a more relaxed brain compared to those who have hunched postures of defeat.

Improving your level of confidence gives you security and has a direct impact on self-esteem.

Self-esteem, unlike what many believe, is not genetic, and it should not depend on others. Increasing your confidence means working on those areas that you think you're not very good at, and the good news is that you can change that starting today!

For all this, I will tell you about my experiences both in terms of self-confidence and trust in relationships with third parties.

Personal story: Training yourself to build self-confidence

Here I am going to tell you about an experience that is really worth framing, because it taught me personally and I want to tell you that if I could do this, there is nothing that you cannot overcome. It was on that path of leaving the comfort zone, and crossing fear to enter into action and success, that I embarked on accepting the invitation of my boss Amy Blair, then SVP HR Global, to give a conference. Not just any conference, the opening conference, where I was invited to present as a success story an innovative flexible benefits plan that we had designed and implemented with my team, which had received 2 awards at the local level, which is why the corporation wanted to review the possibility of implementing it in the rest of the operations in Asia, Europe and the US.

Up to this point we are perfect, at this stage of life I had already surpassed the speaking in public panic attack, I could tell you that I even felt comfortable doing it, I was very seduced by the honor of presenting the project that we had created in Argentina, and that it would be replicated and implemented in the rest of the operations in the

116

world; There was only one detail left: the conference would be in English! Since the participants of the ANNUAL HR GLOBAL MEETING came from different countries with diverse native languages and the common language was English.

I want to tell you that I had studied French during my secondary education, and languages were never an area where I stood out, nor do I have any facility for learning other languages. When the company hired me, bilingual communication had not been a requirement, but with the pace of mergers and acquisitions and shareholding changes, this competency turned out to be must to successfully perform in a position, such as the one I held at that time as HR Senior Vice President, since I had to begin communicating with Native American executives and colleagues, issuing reports and answering questions via email in English. To do this, they gave me intensive training that I took full advantage of! I received individual training for one hour a day and an additional class three times a week with the *controller* and current friend Fernando Melano, who was the same as me in terms of language level and who sweated as

117

much as I did when he had to take on a presentation in a foreign language. Perhaps the only difference with Fernando was that I had one less barrier in making presentations in our language, but at the level of insecurity, this lack of confidence that I have been talking about, we both had it equally developed. I remember long talks we had when we worked on a project together, where we convinced each other about the need to improve that aspect of our development, and a week later we were overwhelmed with work, and with difficulty devoting essential time to improving the English language, and it played tricks on us when it came to putting that skill to the test.

But a new scenario had presented itself, I had received an invitation, a call to give a conference. Of course, one possibility was to excuse myself for not having the language skills required to present the project, or I could put everything into training myself to jump over the line of fear, and enter the zone of action in order to achieve success; Can you imagine what option I took? Yes, yes, I trained, not just 8 hours a week on basic language teaching issues, I also hired language coaching on my own that prepared me in conversation. I prepared, with

118

the help of the team, an incredible presentation, but in addition, with my language coach, we put together some effect tricks with keywords and designed a *speech* that I practiced hundreds of thousands of times! I even recorded it on a CD and listened to it every chance I had: driving every day, going for a run on the weekend, in a bath, even on the plane flight that took me to London, where the meeting it was taking place.

What had me most worried, since I could learn my *speech* and in fact was doing so, were the questions that could surprise me and would not know how to answer, them would panic, and remain absorbed in that situation. But I also prepared that, I asked my Chilean colleagues, with whom we shared an excellent level of camaraderie and who suffered from the language much more than me! They asked me a question, the answer to which I had also rehearsed, and that resource gave me additional security.

To put you in context, my additional surprise came when the car picked me up at Heathrow airport and took me 90 miles to the outskirts of London, where the ANNUAL HR MEETING would take place that year. But you can't imagine what I found when I arrived... a castle! Yes, a castle that had been reconstituted and operated as a hotel. The place was divine, and the feeling was like being inside a story. And in that castle the hundred main executives of the corporation who represented the different operations around the world were present.

The time has finally come! The place where the event took place was in what was previously the hall in which until a hundred years ago the nobility who owned that majestic construction offered their banquets to the British royalty.

Anyway, a great and challenging opportunity to test my confidence! I'm not going to deny that my legs were shaking a little when I had to pass in front of everyone, but I improvised a nice opening where I told them:

Well, I am Marisa Piñeiro, as many of you know I come from Argentina, almost at the end of the world! Before starting the presentation, I would like to share with you an important fact and that is that my parents loved choosing a French school for my education, so... I started studying English just a year ago (I smiled in an honest way and

120

everyone laughed out loud, so at that moment I finished by saying) but! I will do my best! (I took a deep breath and started).

The presentation was a success, and I gained a lot of confidence, and from then on, no one stopped me!

Personal story: Trust in my team

I also have an experience to tell in relation to the trust of my team and towards my team. It was also a very difficult moment in my personal life, which tested me in many aspects and also on a professional level and as a leader.

I was accompanying my partner going through a long and difficult agony, admitted to a sanatorium in Palermo just steps away from the company. I was already exhausted from occupying several difficult, delicate places and at the same time with a high level of emotional and even physical fragility, given that the situation I was experiencing did not allow me to eat or sleep well and worries did not stop invading my mind. Fortunately, I had Alejandro Harrison as my boss, who in addition to being an outstanding professional, is an incredible

121

human being, who gave me the necessary flexibility so that I could handle my duties at a calmer pace and in a more relaxed manner, providing me with his support and covering me in all the aspects that depended on me. But I have a personality of those who commit themselves, who do not get rid of responsibilities, in fact, the opposite happens to me. Fortunately, in addition to a great boss, I had a very good team, to whom I had not delegated enough until that moment, because I did not fully trust their experience, and it was something that they perceived, which is why they also didn't give an A+ delivery, since "Marisa can do everything."

Until Marisa had to deal with another issue more important than her position and corporate responsibilities, she had to accompany her partner and say goodbye to a great love in her life. So without getting depressed and trying to put myself together the day after, admitted to the sanatorium suite where I spent the night with him, after leaving Cala with my parents, I took a shower in the morning, his sister or his mom came to replace me, and I went to work at the company, but without being able to stop thinking for a minute, how he was, what would happen, if he would wake up, if he would call me... then on the third morning, I decided to call my secretary, ask her to organize a virtual meeting with my direct reports, an extra challenge since at that time there were not many technological tools at hand, and she did it! When I logged in, everyone looked at me in a bewildered manner. What was I doing anywhere other than the company at 10 a.m.? And it was the moment when I was vulnerable, I told them about my situation and the absolutely necessary decision I had made, to rely 100% on them to manage the company. I pointed out the critical points, I highlighted each and every one of their strengths, I asked them for mutual collaboration, I also asked them to trust my criteria for assigning some work, I reminded them and reaffirmed the freedom they always had to turn to me for any situation they needed and that is how I managed the operation of the company practically remotely. It was a very sad moment in my life, but where I rescue on a professional level, this tremendous practical lesson that the situation left me, since after that experience, the performance and the relationship with the team was increasingly better.

Clara Campoamor

It was difficult to choose a woman who has left a lesson in relation to trust, since all of them, to a greater or lesser extent, have managed to leave their mark through their trust in themselves, and in the people they relied on to achieve their goal.

But in this case, it is Clara Campoamor who resonates with me as a great reference for trust, who was a prominent Spanish writer, politician and defender of women's rights. She never hid her republican ideals. For this reason, when she was proclaimed in April 1931, she wanted to be in the engine room of the new regime to try to enshrine the democratic principle of equality between men and women. She obtained her seat in the ranks of the Radical Party, actively participated in the commission that drafted the Constitution and defended women's suffrage in a memorable debate in front of 470 men and only one woman, Victoria Kent, who at the last minute renounced her support for reasons of opportunity: women deserved the right but were not yet prepared to

124

exercise it.

It is said that she achieved the vote for Spanish women, but what she did was much more. That woman, on October 1, 1931, managed to establish Spain, for the first time, with full democracy. The only suffragist in the world who achieved it from the tribune of a parliament thanks to those peculiar constituent elections of '31, in which women could not vote, but could be elected. Unfortunately, she died in exile in Switzerland, but faithful to her ideas and very sure of herself, her work and her legacy.

Lack of confidence is a terrible traveling companion. It paralyzes and makes you not even try to fight for what you want so much, so it ends up leaving you locked in a small comfort zone.

Questions for your own reflection

1. *Do you lack self-confidence?*

2. *Does your fear of failure make you miss opportunities again and again?*

3. *Do you fear ridicule? Are you one of those who never asked questions in class and don't do so today in meetings?*

4. *When was the last time you felt afraid of not being able to achieve something?*

5. *What aspects make you feel most vulnerable?*

6. *Do you practice more than once to achieve a goal that is very difficult for you, and where you were took on blame for a failure?*

7. *What situation do you remember, in which you had confidence in yourself? What was it due to?*

8. *What situation do you remember, in which you had complete trust in others? What was the reason?*

Try it! Make a list of things that you don't dare do, simple things, complex things, everyday things, work things, sports things, whatever you want and all kinds of things, and then choose one at a time and try, try, try! Don't be afraid of error, don't be afraid of ridicule, don't be afraid of what people will say about you! Just do it! You'll see how good it feels when you finally get it!

4. COOPERATION / COLLABORATION

"The key to business success is cooperation. Friction slows the progress."
James Cash Penny

"Form a team. Gathering is the beginning. Working together is success."
John C. Maxwell

"Big discoveries and improvements invariably involve cooperation of many minds."
Alexander Graham Bell

Working together is cooperation.

If the word cooperation is divided, we notice that 'co' means together, and 'operation' is a project or work. When we refer to collaboration, we understand it as the process of two or more people or organizations who work together to complete a task or achieve a goal.

Collaboration is similar to cooperation. Most collaboration requires leadership, but a collaborative leadership style and not the top-down and authoritarian type. Daniel Goleman mentions in his book "Resonant Leader" that there is no single type of ideal leadership, but each one of them best applies to a given situation, this is how in moments where you need to right the ship, for example, the Authoritarian leader is the most effective, this is not indicated in other stages of maturation or situations to provide contributions to the team. In the same way as happens with the other styles excellently described by the author, such as the visionary, the coach, the affiliative, the democratic, the example-driven or the authoritarian, each one with its advantages and disadvantages.

Although I fully agree with the author, in my opinion, the most effective leadership is the one we develop respecting our essence and based on our strengths, working in the areas that add to us and that we do not have as developed. Now, there is no doubt that you can go faster alone, but you definitely go further together! And not only further, but also more solid! And based on building more lasting relationships, so it is clear that, at least currently, it is no longer an option for the leader not to seek the advantages of collaboration, cooperation that allows growth, but with others. It is proven that teams that work collaboratively

129

generally access greater resources, recognition, and rewards when faced with competing for finite resources.

It is part of community life, and is especially noticeable in the work, organizational, economic, political, diplomatic and military spheres, among many others.

Thus, cooperation is fundamental for life in society, because it is a better and more efficient way to manage matters based on the collective interest.

Collaborative leadership is definitely the opposite of competitive leadership, whose pace is determined by individual interest.

When a leader bases their management on command and control, and seeks to make teams respond to their needs, they create a culture of discrepancy, looking for blame and division among work teams. Decisions are made authoritatively, above any other alternative that turns out to be better.

On the other hand, if a good idea is shared in an organization, there will be more opportunities to generate value if someone else reviews it, if someone contributes another perspective, an

130

alternative idea or amplifies the development possibilities of the idea and this is achieved through diversity, which is a characteristic advantage of a collaborative culture.

Companies obtain better results when people are prepared to lead their ideas and at the same time support proposals. In addition, they allow for the generation of positive work environments, which improve the individual and collective performance of those who are part of it, largely ensuring a successful future.

When there is collaborative leadership, although the leader makes the final decision, they took into account the different views and opinions of their collaborators.

In this type of leadership, the objective is to create effective solutions, based on the contribution of the different points of view of the collaborators, taking advantage of the experience and knowledge that come together to broaden the perspective of the different analyzes and possible scenarios.

This provides many benefits, such as the contribution of improvements, having options for

131

different solutions for the same problem, generation of opportunities for the business, increased motivation of collaborators, creation of environments and plants of innovation, development of productive and high-quality teams' performance, among the most relevant.

What are the characteristics that allow us to define collaborative leadership?

These are the ones that, in my opinion, I select as keys to identifying that we are in the presence of collaborative leadership. There may be others that complement, but none of those should be missing from the ones I mention below.

- They create collaboration networks, since the leader's desire to have power creates barriers with collaborators and the loss of opportunities for improvement, so to give rise to collaborative leadership, it is necessary to put aside the desire for control. To achieve credibility, you must work as a team, with whom you will find the best alternatives; Thus, collaborators will develop the necessary confidence to participate, contributing their enthusiasm, knowledge and learning.

- They promote the generation of information

132

flows, unlike autocratic leaders, who consider information as power. It is important to understand that to better develop tasks, you must have access to adequate information, since knowing all the variables involved and past experiences helps prevent the same mistakes from being made. In addition, it favors the generation of ideas, contributes to creativity, allows the discovery of competitive advantages, and improves processes, among other advantages.

- They involve its managers in decision-making, allowing themselves the possibility of obtaining the knowledge and perspective that others provide, sharing contextual information with their reports, so that they fully understand the problem, the challenges and the commitments involved in implementing the decision to be taken.

- They manage differences of opinions, combining different perspectives to produce new ideas and alternative solutions. They apply effective communication that fosters openness, allows for the establishment of bonds of trust,

133

and motivates people to give their best. They also make use of emotional intelligence to manage diversity and emotions, converting the feeling that emerges after making mistakes into learning and abandoning frustration and feelings of guilt, which allows maintaining a positive approach to discover opportunities in adverse situations.

- They set shared goals, helping to integrate and motivate the team, since the efforts of each one to make them come true correspond to decisions in which they participated and directly impact the results of each and every one of the team members. Likewise, it creates a culture that develops goals by project, by area and by business unit, always aligned with the general goals of the company.

- They connect global ideas through the experience of each of the team members, under collaborative leadership, helps connect ideas that allow some to be exploited and compensate for others. Understanding what others are going through is essential in collaborative leadership.

- They develop empathy to reach consensus on

decision making. By actively listening and putting yourself in the other person's shoes, you can understand the value of that person's ideas.

- They inspire their collaborators by example, acting in the same way that they ask of those they direct. That means extending collaborative leadership to other levels in the company.

- They influence rather than manipulate, using their experience, knowledge and background to influence others. For example, when agreeing on a decision. The leader's vision is broader and with this argument they help convince their team, while respecting better alternatives.

Therefore, a common aspect of the characteristics of collaborative leadership is that it unifies people's efforts towards a common goal, seeking commonalities and similar points regarding their individual goal, which allows breaking down any potential barriers and achieving self-motivation in each of the team members. Thus, the fact of unifying criteria allows people to participate in achieving collective well-being, allowing others to lead an idea and rotate that role, represents a challenge where the leader must be convinced that they do not lose power, but on the contrary, gains opportunities. Knowing how to listen, practice empathy, act with emotional intelligence, compensate for different personalities, create collaboration networks, requires patience and time, but it is worth it since the diversity of criteria makes it possible to create new ideas and solutions, and how the famous phrase goes "two or more heads are better than one".

And why collaboration, or collaborative leadership?

Because nothing happens one by one, as a team we learn, we enrich ourselves, we develop, we complement each other, and we grow through a great network.

Because in life everything is better as a team, the gaze of another, the hand of a partner, the different vision, the opinion and the discrepancy add up, it makes us better.

Competition takes away, it is an absurd struggle of power, egos and places, which I identify more in the past, but which with the help of new generations we must completely eradicate from organizations.

136

Personal story: The mobilizing force of cooperation

My experience to share in this chapter has to do with a great project that we carried out in the company, launching the entire Media 360 Platform, back in 2007 when everything in this field was absolutely new.

First of all, we bought a small company, with about 27 employees, who had been working on WEB developments and had some interesting products. From the team we rescued the professionals with the most creativity, innovation, knowledge and experience for the creation of Digital Media management. Now, it was all so new, there was so much ignorance in the market, that when we looked for references, metrics, previous cases, we found virgin territory and a lot of improvisation. The team that had joined was diving into new technologies, platforms and developments to apply the strategy we had in mind: take the screen to another place, proposing a new interaction with the viewer.

Maybe today, 13 years ago, everything seems very distant to us, but if you remember, the relationship in the television world was unidirectional, there was a programmer on a channel, whether OPEN or CLOSED TV, where the content was programmed by them and offered at a certain time, and the viewer who wanted to see it had to accommodate their time based on the grid or lose the opportunity to see it. You could like it or not, and the only way that media companies had to test the audience's acceptance was through a measurement system, with the inconsistencies that it offers.

The evolution that the internet universe and technological advancement brought to the media industry is truly wonderful. Now consumers have great accessibility to content, through different screens, they can take advantage of the possibility offered by different streaming platforms, OTT *(Over the Top)*, in addition to several tools that allow consumers to interact with the content, and... as if all this were not enough! the relationship with different social networks such as FB, Twitter and Instagram, which allow us to listen to and learn about the diversity of tastes and opinions of consumers. All this makes it easier to know the audience as the main point when developing any strategy. Interactive images and videos not only serve to interact with users, but at the same time reduce the bounce rate and increase dwell time. At the same time, it is possible to take advantage of the data that is collected to know the tastes that help us generate content that is closer to the viewer, in addition to making advertising segmentation possible.

But I know, I went overboard in this business that I am passionate about! Without boring you with the topic, what I was trying to tell was that we were getting into a new way of making television, which offers many more possibilities, brings enormous opportunities, but also comes with threats that are extremely resisted by the most traditional media entrepreneurs.

And in that context, I was looking to be disruptive in relation to the competition's offering, without much information, without witness cases to show the way and with a great barrier of resistance, both internal and external. So after some failed attempts, we bet on hiring a company that provided the entire service on average, the bet did not work since the provider was very skilled in selling a service and development that did not have the knowledge or the ability to provide, which caused us extreme inconveniences, from the failure to meet goals to the wear and tear of the professionals who internally made up the area.

And there I was 12 months after having made the wrong decision, with the challenge in front of me, pulling my tongue out, a sunk cost in a supplier that turned out to be a failure, a contract of at least 2 years to be able to leave and they are managing all our databases, which caused an enormous contingency and additional risk to manage.

It was in that situation that a moment occurred in which I took a breath and decided to be vulnerable with my team, I asked them for a meeting without an end time, I shared with them all the data, thoughts, information, ideas that I had been considering alone, and I threw the challenge on the table: what if we do it *in house?* What happens if we prepare? If we put together the strategy and the platform? Do we think about contests, positioning tools, marketing campaigns to accompany? Do we copy the database and work silently these months to unhook the supplier when we are ready? Everything indicated that it would be

140

very close to the end of the contract, and we would once again take control of what we had already been learning. But after a year of experimenting and training ourselves by making mistakes, it left us in a place of greater preparation and solidity.

Everyone's eyes lit up, ideas kept appearing, they overlapped with enthusiasm as they shared them among everyone, the team's energy had returned! And not only that, but it had also multiplied exponentially! Now it was time to get to work and so we did! From the area manager to the last layout designer, the programmers, community manager and I, we dedicated additional hours to our general objectives to get to work on this plan! Of course I worked with the team side by side, regardless of the ranks and positions, collaboratively with a clear goal that motivated us to meet, especially towards the end, many times on weekends, we ate pizzas and ice cream and more and more ideas appeared!

The launch was a complete success! The sector is the one that today leads the strategy of the vast majority of new businesses, driving the push towards the convergence of technologies, screens, platforms and formats that allow an infinite number of potential ways to distribute and transmit content to our audiences.

Kathryn Bigelow

The woman I choose to bring in this chapter is Kathryn Bigelow, who was the first woman to win an Oscar for best director for her work on the film *The Hurt Locker*, competing with great film directors like Quentin Tarantino (*Damn bastards*), Lee Daniels (*Precious*) y Jason Reitman (*Up in the Air*). Although, in the history of the Oscars, a woman has been nominated five times in this category, no one before had managed to win the award. Kathryn in various interviews has mentioned that her work would not have been possible and would not have achieved the brilliance that led her to achieve the statuette, without the collaboration of each and every member of the technical team, actors, assistants and creatives, among others.

Questions for your own reflection

1. *Do you feel like you can do everything alone?*

2. *Are you the type to share a good idea when it appears in your mind?*

3. *Do you know how to ask for help? Do you do it frequently? If you don't know how to do it, have you tried to overcome it?*

4. *What satisfies you more, achieving a goal individually or as a team?*

5. *Do you practice your listening?*

6. *Do you think you learn from your colleagues, both those who are similar to you and those who are different, who have different thinking and training?*

7. *Do you consider that the appreciative exchange of our skills and competencies helps your professional development?*

8. *Do you think that as a team the path is easier and the inconveniences are overcome more easily?*

9. *If you had the opportunity, how does it feel to share challenges with a team and have the path of opportunities unblocked?*

SKILLS OF COURAGE

"When there is Courage, you live. When there is no Courage, you survive."

Ingrid Rivera

On many occasions I heard that having courage is interpreted as synonymous with bravery, however, it is not the correct meaning. Courage is not the opposite of fear, but it is fear that drives a person to generate courage and this situation puts them into action and makes them the protagonist of their life. While that person who fails to activate courage is said to survive, because they are inundated by fears and limiting beliefs.

5. COURAGE

To be a good leader and advance our goals, it is essential to have or develop that amount of courage that allows us to take steps, small or big, but that drive us to do, and that doing gives us the energy to work on our own growth, as well as that of the companies, areas or teams that we direct.

Courage is facing a great challenge, where everything indicates that we have absolutely everything against us, where the bet is 9 to 1 that we lose the battle, where that battle seems very difficult, where we are very alone, and in which we have cold sweats alone when we think about what's coming... but even so, we go out on the field and we leave with the conviction that we are going to achieve it!

Personal story: The growth that courage leaves you

The experience I have to share now to you is tragicomic (tragic and comic), like many of the

147

experiences I go through in this book, nothing more and nothing less than life itself.

It was towards the end of 2009, the corporation had sold the majority of the shareholding of the company in which I worked as SVP of HR and the goal of the new shareholders was to make the operation more efficient, merging the company's payroll with resources that they brought from other companies, part of the new shareholder group that were working in other countries.

Of course, in these cases, unions go into a state of alert anywhere in the world, but especially in Argentina and at a time when the context did not help since we were going through a major economic crisis.

I remember that we were in a meeting with the shareholders, on the top floor of the company, located in the Palermo Hollywood neighborhood, reviewing the plans that the new shareholders who had just taken control proposed to carry out. Suddenly you begin to hear disturbances in the street, sirens, screams and sounds of drums, which alarms the foreigners, alien to the folklore of union demonstrations in our country, who were directing

148

the presentation. So, I go out to see my secretary, asking if she knows what it is about, and she invites me to look out on the terrace. As we headed together to the balcony that my office had in front of Honduras Street, he informed me that the union representatives and many employees of our company, along with others who are in solidarity with these causes, had blocked the pedestrian access street to the company, and through the garage, they organized a rubber burning and had gathered more than 1,000 people with flags, protesting for a supposedly just cause.

Looking down, I see how intimidating the situation was given the fervor and agitation of these people. I noticed that they were already beginning to improvise grills to prepare the famous "chorizos", a must in this type of mobilization, a sign of their intentions not to leave the place for a long period of time. Our meeting, which had already been going on for 4 hours, was about to end and just thinking that the shareholders had to return to the hotel through that crowd, seemed like an unimaginable scenario.

I enter the room again, I observe their gazes

149

towards me full of fear and anxiety, expectant of my account of the situation that was being experienced at the door of the offices. And there I found myself, as always, being the only woman at the table, with the responsibility of achieving the objective of reducing payroll, leading the cultural change with the new resources that were added to the company, internalizing in that meeting what ambitious of some goals, in terms of time, costs, brand impact and operation impact and additionally now with the double challenge of having to guarantee the transfer of executives from the company to their hotel while preserving their physical integrity.

I explained to them that the commotion was the product of a union mobilization, and I described the context we had at the door of the building, but I minimized the issue somewhat to prevent the gentlemen from running away.

They made clear in their expression the great question that my management generated in them. I read in their knowing glances at each other, in their gestures and body language, their great doubt, that I, a blonde woman 1.55 cm tall and 47 kg, could achieve the goal successfully, at least in the terms

150

in that they had raised it.

The CEO, present at the same meeting, with whom I was a co-team for more than a decade and who knew many of my *skills* and experience, although trusted my efficiency, was doubtful about the ambitiousness of the goal that had been established on the board that they had just presented to us.

Therefore, he began to object, especially the *deadline* and expected impacts, with a logical foundation, citing context, market practices, previous experiences and those of other companies... and... while Alejandro spoke, I perceived in the eyes of the executives the construction of prejudice, which said: "this duo is not capable to carry out a tremendous challenge."

Logically, American executives have a lot of experience in various aspects, but if there is a field that they underestimate for not having a background like ours, it is in relation to the processes of reengineering and closing companies and the management of unions in Argentina. Then, I interrupted the first executive who was responding to Alejandro's objections, and with complete firmness I emphatically confirmed that I would lead the project and that despite the enormous challenge it represented, as the CEO was trying to explain, I was going to achieve it, all Men in the room looked at me absorbed and at that moment I only limited myself to transmitting courage and security.

Now I had to think about how I could get them out of that place without scratches and as the situation presented itself, it was going to take a couple of hours for the waters to calm down. As the afternoon was ending and taking advantage of the American custom of dining early, I improvised with the help of my efficient secretary a dinner on site, which allowed us to advance in the definition of many *next steps*, work on the bond and understanding with the new shareholders, and also, as planned, buy time until the crowd that had gathered at the place disperses and thus guarantee the safe retirement of everyone.

Needless to say, while driving home the cold sweat appeared, but in those moments, I sought to think about the ideas that would allow me to unblock the inconveniences that arose in achieving the objective that this new challenge put in front of

152

me and that I sought to achieve.

This is how, on this occasion and on each of the others in which I pushed my courage to cross a new zone of challenge, I felt a development, a growth, a change that makes room for the creation of a new self, one bigger, more solid and experienced.

Courage in our lives appears on different occasions, many times reactively, other times proactively, when I seek to overcome a challenge despite not presenting an extreme situation, like the case I just told you, going through it and overcoming it generates in me a more solid and expert woman.

I could have negotiated more time, more budget, but I would not have had the opportunity to show them, but above all, show myself what I am capable of doing.

Courage turns us on and also allows us to prove to ourselves that we can.

At this point, you are surely wondering the result of this act of courage that I just told you, right? Well, I tell you that the objective was achieved and over time I earned the respect and trust of the new shareholders.

Personal story: Bodyguard of the new CEO

And speaking of courage, I have to tell you this short story, but... worth it!

In the last sale of the company, a new Spanish CEO had been assigned to lead the Spanish-speaking business in America and Spain, who, unlike the American executives, claimed to have experience in managing unions and large strike scenarios in the companies that he had led in Spain in the past.

Only he and I had attended the office of one of the *buffet* of lawyers that we were evaluating hiring to accompany our restructuring project.

The reason why we moved was to avoid the leak of rumors, considering how delicate the situation was and how easy it would have been for the employees to make conjectures if they saw the three most recognized studios in the field of outsourcing parading through our meeting room. So it was that mid-morning, we left with my car towards downtown, and found the fenced area precisely in the place where we were going, which

154

is why I decided to leave the car in a parking lot approximately ten blocks away and walk the rest of the way.

We arrived without difficulty at the studio and had a long meeting that lasted more than two hours. This place was located on Av. Belgrano and Av. 9 de Julio in the heart of downtown, and we had to return to the parking lot in Moreno almost Av. Callao, the only drawback was that by the time we left the meeting, the fervor of the riot was huge, you can get an idea, dozens of buses parked on the avenues, groups of workers from left-wing political parties, led by hooded men, flags, flares, drums, soup kitchens, chants, alcoholic beverages and also marijuana.

Eduardo suggests that we stay for lunch in the area because it was impossible to cross the avenue. It was already close to 2 in the afternoon, so we headed opposite of the riot, and found a hotel where we ate some salads while we reviewed the main points of the meeting we had held with the lawyers, and we planned the questions that we would do to the next team of professionals with whom we met the next day.

Being 3 p.m., I suggest to go look for the car to head back to the company, where we had to continue attending to our agenda. At that moment he asks me if I consider that the riots have stopped, to which I answer that almost certainly not, because in general the riots occur between 5 p.m. and 6 p.m.

We left and the panorama was just as complicated as an hour and a half before. He suggested that I take a taxi to the office and leave my car in the parking lot, but we waited for 20 minutes, and no available taxi was moving around the area. So, I took a deep breath and said, 'Let's go to the parking lot! You follow me with a quick and firm step and in 15 minutes we are in the car back to Palermo!' He tries to convince me otherwise, but he really didn't see alternatives and he also had to attend to a complicated agenda in his two remaining days in Buenos Aires, so, without being convinced, he agreed to my suggestion.

Of course, I was sweating while I prayed and hoped that everything would go well, imagine the situation... an executive in a European design suit and me with my tailleur and matching stilettos, crossing in the middle of the mass of angry people

156

over a claim of social inequalities. But we arrived safely at the car, and from there straight to the company to finish another long day.

He didn't mention anything during the trip to the company, but upon arriving he told me, 'Honestly, I value your courage to handle yourself in these contexts, despite experiencing strikes in Spain, I have never been in similar situations, now I feel absolutely comfortable that you are the one leading the restructuring.'

Malala Yousafzai

As a reference for a woman with courage who left her mark on this world, I chose Malala Yousafzai, who at only 17 years old and after being shot in the head while returning home by bus from school, continued the fight for women worldwide. Malala was a victim of the Taliban regime, which in Pakistan prohibits girls from attending school. She differed from the general attitude of women who decided to confine themselves to their homes. For this reason, she was awarded the Nobel Peace Prize.

Questions for your own reflection

1. *What is the level of courage in each of us? What is your level of courage?*

2. *Are you born with courage?*

3. *Can courage be trained?*

4. *Do women have less courage than men? Or is it the other way around?*

5. *Do you think you have courage? Why?*

6. *Could you remember a situation where you felt angry?*

7. *Do you think you lack courage? Why?*

8. *Could you remember a situation where you lacked courage?*

9. *¿What things could you modify in the future to test your courage?*

6. COMMITMENT

"Commitment is what turns a promise into reality." *Abraham Lincoln*

This ability is very important and valued by companies and leaders, those of us who have it innate or developed almost naturally, we are unable to measure the importance and power it has.

What is commitment? A commitment is something that has to be fulfilled, a tacit or explicit agreement between two parties with the aim of achieving an end.

Commitment is defined as the bond of loyalty, through which an individual decides to remain in respect for people or things, whether it is their word, their thoughts, commitment to their parents, their children, society and even their superior or the company where they work.

While affective commitment refers to emotional association, when an employee's commitment is to the firm they work for, we are talking about work

159

commitment.

What exactly do we mean by work commitment? It occurs when the commitment of workers is reflected in their intellectual and emotional involvement with the company, and they provide their personal contribution to achieve the success of the business.

Considering that commitment determines the productivity of employees in many aspects, and consequently impacts the performance of companies, this is the reason why it is a skill so sought after by leaders and companies. It is the famous *engagement* that companies incorporate into their indicator boards as objectives, sometimes erroneously attributing them only to the human resources areas.

Personally, the commitment that I assume in various aspects is given by that dedication that makes me leave 200% of myself no matter how tired I may be, no matter what other topic or activity I am postponing in pursuit of accomplishing what I pledged my word for, to achieve what I committed myself to.

When we seek to achieve *engagement* in our

160

employees, we must make them feel happy in their workplace, making them feel aligned and connected with the company, its mission and its leaders, in order to increase their sense of well-being. And because of this feeling, countless improvements are generated such as increased productivity, decreased absenteeism rates and even reduced conflict.

Getting employees to commit to the company requires committing to them, allowing them to grow, involving them in the organization's projects, listening to them and seeking their well-being in every possible way.

Among the practices that allow developing and managing employee commitment, I can highlight the following as key:

- Gain the trust of employees and trust them.
- Never promise things that we are not sure we can keep.
- Speak clearly and encourage transparency.
- Welcome the team and accompany a *soft landing* with a good induction.
- Always communicate, avoiding the proliferation of rumors.

161

- Improve the quality of life of individuals whenever possible.
- Recognize effort and work well done.

In my case, the commitment that I assume in myself has to do with sweating the shirt and the example, the values, rules and practices with which I operate, are those that I then ask of the reports that I have known how to lead, the teams that I have had the opportunity to create and in many cases the honor to direct.

Personal story: The move

In this chapter, I have a story to tell you and it has to do with that, with a great challenge that everyone doubted about completing and that I shouldered, after having some meetings with those involved in the project and convening my team, indicating the north of the sought goal, and the expected level of expectations.

The challenge was to make the building's move in record time, without affecting business continuity, generating cost savings, improving operational efficiency, reducing risks and contingencies, and achieving an excellent work environment in the new work location.

162

It was the month of January when we received the news that the owner of the building where we had 75% of the company operating had sold the property. Oh, and to a television company that competes with ours! ☹

I immediately began to put together the strategy and get moving, finding out alternatives to put them on the decision board, estimating budgets and analyzing the pros and cons of each of them. They ranged from complete properties to rent, buildings to finish, or to build from the ground up, with and without a recording studio, in short, an interesting number of alternatives.

By then, the other 25% of the Buenos Aires operation, which included the technique and a programming and *in house* (creative department), was set up in a 1000 m2 apartment, in a 3-story building that we shared with 2 other companies, 100 meters from the building that we had to leave in just 8 months.

This is how, after contacting more than 7 real estate agencies in the area that work on that target of buildings, visiting nearly 18 properties, and driving around the entire area of the audiovisual hub completely, to have the tax benefit offered by developing the activity in that sector of the city, we looked at buildings with a recording studio, without a studio, with up to 3000 m2 (which was the amount we left), 4000 m2 and 5000 m2 and more to centralize the operation in a single place, considering Business expansion within 2 years. Anyway, raking work they call it.

Now, I couldn't help but take into account that the separation that we currently had between buildings was 100 m away, and despite the risk generated by having employees walking between one building and another, that was all the complication and the greater risk that could be presented; while by moving 15/30 minutes from the current location, the operation became less efficient and riskier.

The directors' garage was in the shared building and one night when I was going to pick up my car to go home, I ran into Mariano Chiade, owner of the Mandarina production company, who had rented the third floor of that building, and after greeting him, I told him that I was looking to rent meters among other alternatives in case he knew anything, so he could let me know.

164

In parallel with the management of the company, at that time from my position as COO (Chief Operations Officer), I was constantly thinking and reviewing alternatives that would find a solution that had to meet several requirements, be economically viable, operationally efficient, rapid implementation and ensuring business continuity at all times.

The following week, I received a call from Chiade, who suggested that we meet to review an option that he had discussed with his partner. The proposal was to advance his departure from the building, which had another year of contract, charging an amount that he required to enter another building that was more convenient for his logistics, and we could condition it in that time, together with the ground floor of the same building, which was unoccupied and where we already had the first floor, with a remaining term in the rental contract of about 14 months from the date.

The proposal seemed very reasonable, together with the CEO and CFO we analyzed numbers, alternatives and requested a meeting with the owners of the property, with whom we maintained an excellent relationship, in addition to impeccable conduct as clients regarding the care of the building and compliance with the pay.

They were interested in the proposal to finalize the rental of the building with us (for almost two more years another company would remain on the 2nd floor). But those three floors provided enough meters for the business development context in three years and in the future, we could think about growing in this other place in the same building, which was originally a warehouse with renovations in its construction to which there were to prepare for the operation of companies with service activities.

Also, something that I loved was that it had a hidden exit to the garage, which allowed us to go out safely in times of union conflicts, haha!

We work on the project design, calculate the economic impact and present it along with the top 5 other options to shareholders in a video conference. They approved the alternative ranked first by us and from there they operated in record time to reach the *deadline*.

166

The GANTT was extremely tight, so monitoring was almost daily.

We hired the Contract company for the design and turnkey delivery work, but the times were so complicated that despite deciding to work on weekends for 6 months, we had to take care of several logistical issues as a company.

In addition to the daily management of the business, I dedicated myself to leading this project and mobilizing the commitment of a large number of people, on the one hand a group of professionals from the Contract company, such as Alejandro Mariani, Marina Mirabelli and Ximena Torres, I also had my entire team of leaders who were committed day to day alongside me, the maintenance manager, whose leadership was truly a challenge in itself, and the managers and employees of the Atlas moving company. And even my daughter, who was only 8 years old at the time, assumed a leadership role in the move; helping the movers who unloaded the furniture, technology and other elements, to place them in the places assigned for each position, given that prior coordination work had been carried out, identifying the different desks with specific coding. Everyone marveled at seeing her just over a meter tall, carrying the coded plans in her hand and pointing out the location to visit. They told me 'With that attitude you can't deny that she is your daughter!'

My commitment was such that I remember those days that required me to carry out the driving, very intense and at the same time extensive days, days that began before dawn and ended late at night, but even so they were not enough, which took me to invest even the weekends where I had to allocate them to the purchase of some furniture and supervision of the progress of construction among other tasks and responsibilities.

A psychologist once told me that after the death of a loved one, moving is the second stress factor that people go through, and as a leader, I knew that this would surely happen to everyone under my leadership. That is why we were concerned, together with my most direct reports, in the production of a welcome pack for employees; who on a Thursday left their offices in a building, with everything packed and labeled (following the specific instructions of the moving company that

168

was in charge of these big moves) to receive them on Monday with their new personalized workplace, in the new building, now with all areas concentrated in the same place and strategically located by floor.

We bought pencil holders that we had engraved with the company logo, a chocolate for each of them, we coordinated a welcome breakfast in the new place that we previously decorated with balloons. That weekend I was with my team, in turn the managers of each area showed up to see how their spaces were being prepared and collaborate on any adjustments. The maintenance area assisted with all the unforeseen events that always arise. The systems area was present taking care of all the connections, with the design area we worked on the communication and signage campaign, and thus each one contributed their grain of sand, as if it were their own home, everyone putting the best of themselves. That's what I call commitment to the company, to a project and above all to people!

Needless to say, it was a complete success!

Valentina Tereshkova

Which woman to choose if I think about commitment? ... many women left their mark showing an unparalleled commitment to their ideals, but I want to choose Valentina Tereshkova, the Soviet woman who was the first woman in history to travel to space and do so alone, in 1963, assuming the commitment to demonstrate to the world the courage of women to be part of a study that sought to answer the question of whether women offered the same physical and mental resistance in space as men. The conclusion after the three days that the extraterrestrial journey lasted was affirmative.

Questions for your own reflection

1. *What does commitment mean to you?*

2. *Do you handle yourself with commitment in your life?*

3. *What value do you give to commitment?*

4. *What prevents you from being committed?*

5. *Do you demand the same level of commitment from others as the one you demonstrate?*

6. *What topics or things do you feel committed to?*

7. *What do you think you should be committed to, and you are not? Why is that?*

8. *Has commitment allowed you to achieve any goal you were pursuing?*

7. CONSTANCY

"I am convinced that half of what separates successful entrepreneurs from unsuccessful ones is pure perseverance."

Steve Jobs

"Winners never quit, and quitters never win."

Vince Lombardi

Consistency, what great skill!

To achieve the things we long for, it is key that we be constant. It is a practice that we develop throughout life, we have been taught it and we teach it to our children, however, and even though it is easy to do, it is still something that is difficult for us to implement on many occasions or sustain in the future.

We all live in situations where we simply have not been consistent, we start something and soon abandon it. It costs us, it is difficult for us, we get frustrated by results that do not come as quickly as we would like, and we simply give up.

What happens to us in the private sphere also happens with leaders, since they are no different from us, I mean in the sense that it is easy for them to be constant in goals or projects they propose, however, they resolve to be so.

It is important to be able to identify a quality common to most great leaders, which consists of developing a philosophy: never give up on established and agreed upon goals, even though this means making great sacrifices of all kinds, mental, emotional and physical. Since they are aware that the price to pay for perseverance is always less than the benefits that are achieved by continuing to persist.

For that same reason, each day, they take the previously assigned step to move forward with any personal commitment they have made.

So, if they decided to do exercises every morning, they write it down in their agenda, set an alarm to remind them, and when the time comes, regardless of whether they had a business dinner or a family celebration, they get up and do the scheduled exercise. Whether it's 15', 30' or 60 minutes, they do it and fulfill their personal commitment more than anything else.

If it is reading, they read for the time they agreed to do so and they also fulfill their commitment. If it is learning a language, exactly the same thing happens, and so on with each of the goals that are proposed.

Therefore, a personal commitment has nothing more to do with themselves, and how it is essential to fulfill them, because they simply put in double, triple or quadruple effort and more if necessary.

In fact, if you cannot be consistent with reading, even if it is only 15 minutes a day, developing the habit of reading, your mentality will not acquire the necessary strength to carry out other major tasks that require your perseverance from start to finish.

Consistency is essential for leaders since the impact is direct to profitability.

Most people falter when it comes to being consistent with something, but my wish is that you continue to persevere in what you want most, that you continue believing that it is possible, and that that desire drives you to never stop, even when you think that you don't have air, that you fall asleep on

174

your desk or that you don't have 100% capacity in a board meeting.

When we are constant, another invaluable characteristic is created, the famous *cruising speed* which they usually identify as the locomotive that advances without stopping; Therefore, always remember this: try hard and don't give up, because when you get there, it is almost impossible not to finish what you started!

Navy SEALs,

There is a curious fact that the *Navy SEALs*, or United States Marine Commandos, considered by many to be the best special operations force in the world, use, and it is what they call the "40% Rule," which means that the moment you think you have given your capacity limit, you are actually using 40%. Therefore, you still have another 60% that you can use.

So, when they are doing their training and they reach a point where mentally, emotionally and physically they think they can't take it anymore, they remember that they are only at 40% of their capacity and they keep going. This concept, based on scientific studies, is what helps them stay alive in extreme stress operations where they are captured by the enemy or are about to die.

The interesting thing is that this rule is not only valid for *Navy SEALs*, but for each and every one of us.

Critical factor of great leaders

Being consistent is the most important critical success factor I have ever known, and it is a characteristic in all great leaders so we must develop it to the maximum. Only in this way can we achieve everything we have imagined and for which we are fighting every day.

So, my recommendation is that you be the leader you have to be and make consistency essential for yourself.

In fact, I have spent a lot of time researching important skills to be an excellent leader, and in this regard, I was greatly surprised when reading and hearing from different experts, who although many put the difference in intelligence, in reality the most important skill is the experience that comes with practice. But above all it is in consistency, and so

176

much so that when a teacher with many years of experience is asked what they see in young people between 25 and 35 years old to know if they are going to be great leaders, their answers are always: your perseverance...

The power of practice

In an experimental room they give as instructions the production of a certain piece. They inform the members of one half of the class that they will measure their grade by the best piece made and the members of the other half, they tell them that they will measure it by the amount of weight of pieces produced; Therefore, the first group investigates, goes to museums, projects, sketches and begins to produce a week prior to delivery. The second group, from the moment they received the instructions, was dedicated the entire time to producing pieces of all types: small, smaller, medium, large and very large to achieve the objective of being qualified for a good total weight of produce pieces.

The surprising thing was that the best piece of the entire course was made by the team that produced in quantity, because so much practice in

177

assembling the pieces allowed them to develop the skill of producing pieces, while the group that was evaluated by its quality, they went into production 5 days before delivery!

Personal story: From recycling to the Media Sustainability strategy

Here I wanted to bring an absolutely graphic anecdote!

One of the reasons why I seek to occupy decision-making positions is precisely because of the opportunity it gives me to have the discretion to make decisions that allow me to change the world, even a little, from my place of influence, but the satisfaction that I get generates that feeling, it translates to a level of happiness that has no comparison.

This is how from my position as COO, depending on me all areas of the company except finance, I begin to design a first guideline of CSR (Corporate Social Responsibility) actions.

It was the year 2006, we were not going through an excellent year in terms of results, and I also already knew by heart what the management of

178

budget allocations to new projects was like. So, I was not willing to waste energy in a battle that I knew I would lose, but... I would not be satisfied with leaving my idea unrealized, even if this took me more than one period, and that's how I started.

While formalizing an agreement with the P. Garraham Foundation, to whom we had begun donating paper for recycling two years ago, I began educating myself in this area. I began measuring the company's carbon footprint, which consists of measuring the business's activities on the environment. In addition, we entered into an agreement with IARSE (Argentine Institute of Corporate Social Responsibility) with whom we exchanged dissemination in exchange for receiving training and *know-how* in the implementation of the project. I promoted the change of the company's lighting to LED, I made agreements with several non-profit organizations that sought to disseminate topics that were also of interest to our company, such as the Argentine Advertising Council, Red Cross, Luchemos por la Vida, Los Piletones, UNICEF, among others. I also formed a volunteer team with those employees who sought to develop activities that allowed them to align their personal interests in relation to improving the environment. And so, from the sum of agreements, the joining of more people, the contribution of more funds and the excellent repercussions on the internal climate, added to the impact of the brand outside the company, four years later I managed to formalize the area. In 2010, I summoned a professional who had extensive experience in CSR issues and appointed her as head of the sector, a great addition that undoubtedly added a lot of value. I delegated to her the comprehensive management of the strategic media sustainability matrix. And in 2012, we managed to publish our first Annual Sustainability Report, where we reported the entire path, we had traveled, with indicators, ratios and definition of new goals.

He was presented to journalists and interested audiences in the Malba auditorium. The Regional CEO who opened the presentation surprised me by recognizing the constant ant path, very constant, that I had done and that had taken us to that place of honor for both him and the company.

It was a great pride for me at that moment to remember that commitment that I made more than six years ago and those first steps with the intention

180

of leaving my mark without knowing how far we would go. Added to this and the perseverance with which we approached each and every action carried out from the beginning, I had the satisfaction of being part of the *Sustainability International Committee*.

Marie Curie

In relation to this important skill such as consistency, perseverance, and not giving up, I want to choose Marie Curie.

There is no scientist in history who has surpassed Marie Curie, the discoverer of Polonium and Radium as chemical elements, in recognition and fame. She went hungry and cold, and risked her health in order not to give up her research passion and worked constantly and tirelessly day after day until she achieved it.

What Marie Curie also left behind was, being able to become rich with her discoveries, she refused to patent the process of isolating radium, leaving it at the disposal of the scientific community.

All in all, it can be said that she fulfilled her

dream: she was the first woman to become a professor at the University of Paris and the first to win the Nobel Prize, shared with her husband Pierre Curie, for their research on radioactive elements.

This is why perseverance is an extremely important skill to achieve objectives and does not require any special knowledge, but on the contrary, it requires work, dedication and discipline, a lot of discipline!

So, I invite you to list your goals, establish tactics and an execution plan to achieve them, because doing so is a guarantee of obtaining it.

Questions for your own reflection

1. How do you proceed when faced with goals that are difficult to achieve?

2. How much do you resist in complicated situations?

3. How long are you willing to stay firm towards your goals?

4. Are you comfortable with your current situation? Do you want to give it a 180-degree turn?

5. Are you clear about what exactly you are pursuing?

6. What is your goal?

7. Are you restless and anxiety doesn't allow you to stop always thinking about another goal?

8. How much do you sweat your shirt to achieve that goal?

---
8. CORPUS

"Your body is a temple from nature and of divine spirit. Keep it healthy;
respect it; study it; grant it it's rights."
Henri-Frédéric Amiel

"The body is the instrument of the soul."
Aristotle

Through self-knowledge and personal development work we can take the step to "create a world in which people want to belong", as Gilles Pajou said.

When we lead, we also put our body.

We expose ourselves all the time, with our body and our emotions.

A great challenge, which is generally subconsciously ignored, is taking care of and feeding the body and soul with positive stimuli.

In this chapter I invite you to reflect on the way we lead ourselves, and what we call self-leadership, since this is the first step we must take when we

184

propose to work on human development.

Starting with self-knowledge, we can analyze several dimensions, how do we lead our emotions? What do we do when we are angry, helpless, afraid, sad? Are we able to discern in our actions whether we have managed appropriately or are we trapped in an emotional impulse?

What if we think about our health? How do we take care of our little ailments? we pay attention to them, or do we leave them "due to lack of time" until the body gives us a more severe call for attention?

How do we manage affection with our partner, family, friends, co-workers, social environment, sports, religion, among others? How do we express joy, sadness, anger?

Are we really aware of our capabilities and abilities and how we can use them to improve our environment and make it more pleasant?

And about our weaknesses? Do we have a plan to turn them into opportunities to improve ourselves?

I understand that the challenge lies in the

motivation that drives us to promote lifelong learning aimed at our personal development in a comprehensive way, that is, taking into account the different human dimensions: whether biological, psychological, social and spiritual. Which leads us to go through our lives as free, authentic people, with self-confidence and strength.

Personal history: Executive and mother

Therefore, in this chapter I chose to tell you two experiences, each of them exposed my body in a different way, but with a strong impact in both cases.

I'm going for the first one, that, at least from a distance, is very funny! Even though it felt strong, destabilizing and difficult to deal with at the time it happened.

I had been Candelaria's mother for less than three months, and I began to attend the company two or three times a week to attend relevant decision meetings or, as in this case, carry out a negotiation.

I remember that I had between 45 minutes to 90 minutes of travel, by car, from home to the

186

company, depending on road works, road closures due to protests or traffic jams due to an accident or simply being stuck in traffic on rush hour.

I tried not to be at the company for more than 4 hours, which, adding the travel time, could leave me absent from my house and away from my daughter for approximately 6 hours.

That day, in addition to closing the coverage of a management position in the sales area, I had to attend a meeting with Citibank corporate to carry out the negotiation of an important package of *payroll* together with the CFO of the company.

I will never forget that it was to be held at 12:30 and at 12:40 they announced that they were on their way, but that they would arrive with a delay of approximately 30 minutes. At that time, I was going through the breastfeeding period and while the negotiation was going on, I felt that the nipple covers were getting wetter and wetter. I had a fitted black ¾ sleeves t-shirt, which I noticed was getting damp as the minutes went by, and then I felt that it was starting to get wet; so I would then covertly try to cover myself with the sheets that I had in front of me on the meeting table.

187

We were in the main room, sitting at the board table where we were on one side Horacio, who was the CFO at that time, and I, while facing each other were the four directors of Citibank, almost needless to say, as in most cases, all men. At one point, in the most fervent of the discussion, I speak, in a firm and elevated tone and right at that moment! A parabola-shaped jet of milk shoots out of my left breast, rising and falling past the middle of the table, almost reaching the sheets that were in front of the Regional Director of *Salesforce* at Citibank.

Their faces! I swear you couldn't imagine those faces in two lifetimes. The CFO, who was about 15 years older than me, managed to look for a box of disposable tissues that he handed me, with his left hand, without looking me in the eyes, so that I could dry myself and with his right hand he dried the table, while he called the service cleaning staff to sanitize everything and offer coffee to relax the atmosphere generated by the accident caused by my breastfeeding condition.

I take advantage of that moment to go to the bathroom to change my protectors and then return to the meeting, resuming the conversation and

188

closing the negotiation, in the terms in which we had set, which was obtaining for our employees all the benefits that exceeded what offered by commercial banks to the market, and at zero cost (it is worth clarifying that the situation was not common at that time, but rather companies paid a cost to the banks for the benefit packages provided to each of the employees).

Years passed and the CFO kept remembering that situation, embarrassing for him, not for me. In my case, the situation only raised an alarm signal for me, regarding this type of multitasking roles that I developed, automatically and almost unconsciously exchanging the different roles in my life: as a professional, mother, partner, daughter, colleague, friend, etc. And the degree of intensity that we put into everything, which makes the body emit its signal to manifest itself, in this case through a jet of breast milk...

Another personal story: Taking care of your health

The following experience that I share with you is not funny, but it is worth telling as a sample of what I have been delving in this chapter about our body.

189

It was a Friday morning, I was in my office with the brand-new Regional Marketing Director, based in Miami, who, after we finished the *meeting call* with an event provider and before entering the next meeting, goes to the bathroom and when she returns, she takes a deep breath and tells me: I have to tell you something! She had arrived in Buenos Aires on Monday morning, we had shared four long and intense days, I like to be a good hostess and in addition to working between 10 and 12 hours straight, I used to invite my colleagues to dinner or to see some place that they might find attractive in Buenos Aires, in short, I treat them how I like to be treated when I am a visitor.

She insists 'I have to tell you!'. 'Yes', I say, 'Of course, tell me whatever it is that has you so upset and worried'. Then, she takes another strong, deep inhalation and asks me 'Have you had the colored nevus that you have on the left side of your forehead checked?', to which I answer yes. She asks again, 'How long ago?'. I remember and make calculations taking into account Cala's age and I answer, 'About 10 or 11 years ago'. She asks me a new question 'And do you check it periodically?', to which I respond 'Well, no, because they never

190

told me that I should do it'.

Her facial expression changes and she tells me 'Look, my mother is an oncologist specializing in skin cases in the USA and there is a statistic that she always mentions and unfortunately she shows me patients and tells me that those who have colored nevus, in the 98% of cases have skin cancer'.

Although I try not to lose my cool, my gaze evidently transforms. She tells me 'Of course I'm not mentioning this to worry you, but to make you take care of yourself! You are an incredible, loving, professional woman, struggling alone with a still young daughter and you deserve to be well! Listen to me and have a good dermatologist check you up'.

I thank her and we enter the other *call* five minutes later, and while this one happens, my mind was in the stratosphere and had sent two messages to ask for help with a medical appointment. My secretary arranged for me to see a dermatologist at 2:30 p.m. that same day, so I took a taxi between meetings to attend to the advice they had just given me.

I arrive at the office, the doctor shows me in almost without delay, I tell her the reason for my consultation, she asks me a series of questions and tells me to take off all my clothes and lie down on the stretcher. I tell her that it was the nevus on my forehead that I wanted to control and in an imperative tone she tells me 'I have to control it, please undress!'

With modesty, I lie down naked on the stretcher and with a giant magnifying glass she begins to examine each part of my body. It is worth clarifying that I am not a person who has many moles, but it still took a good amount of time to examine me, or at least I felt that. Now, the surprise came when she reached my left leg, on the outside of it and almost reaching the ankle, where I had a huge, irregularly shaped mole, her reaction was surprising and worrying. I lift my torso off the stretcher, look at her and say, 'I have something wrong!', she answers 'I cannot diagnose with a simple check-up, but I send you with a letter of recommendation so that you can urgently see the skin oncologist specialist, so that he can evaluate and perform a biopsy of the mole'. She says 'Urgent! Don't forget it'.

Of course, on the way back, I didn't know where
192

I was, it was like stepping on air. I met with Sebastián, my recent boyfriend, who helped me get an appointment ASAP. The one we managed to obtain was for the following Tuesday at 12:00 p.m. You can only imagine what that weekend was like! I couldn't stop thinking about my only daughter, my parents, the future, what would happen to me? Would I get over it? How were my parents going to take it? I had gone through the loss of my partner just 5 years ago, due to fulminant lung cancer, in short, many emotions...

Tuesday arrives, I go to the clinic, a doctor from the Doctor's team sees me, I tell him the whole episode and he has a reaction quite similar to the dermatologist. Observing his reaction, I beg to know what I have, if I am advanced or not, what chances of life, everything! He tells me that it could be anything from a benign mole, which he almost ruled out due to its appearance, to a melanoma in situ, to having involved lymph nodes or metastasis, but that to find out they had to do an excision and send it to pathology.

They performed the procedure on me that same afternoon and I went through the longest fifteen days of my life! Anxiously awaiting the results of the exam.

After getting the results, upon getting in the taxi I opened the report and read that it said: "Vienna Grade V melanoma" since I did not understand what it was referring to, I did what is not recommended to do: search for its meaning in Google. The answer to my search meant that it was the most aggressive and fastest-spreading cancer. Overcome with anguish, I call the doctor, who had kindly given me his cell phone, and he tells me to check if it said, "free margins." Of course, it didn't mention it and he insisted that I look in the report and I desperately read it aloud, but it wasn't there! How awful! The pathology reporting team had forgotten to type it in and that changed my outlook radically!

I overcame that terrible situation, then others came, I was lost at times, anguished, worried, sad, but never devastated and always with hope and positive energy that allowed me to connect with my desire for enjoyment and life.

But I learned a lesson in the most accelerated course of my life, and that lesson is the one I want

194

to share with you. Regardless of the amount of responsibilities you have on your back, your position, your children, parents, siblings, economic situation, problems, and dozens of other issues, **nothing, and I mean nothing,** is more important than your body and your soul, and it requires a lot of care to be good with you primarily and then so that you can offer the best of yourself to the rest.

Helen Keller

I have chosen a great woman as the most representative female exponent for this chapter. Helen Keller was born in the United States in 1880, and is recognized as a leading writer, speaker and political activist. You may wonder what made Hellen so special that I chose her for this chapter. Hellen suffered a serious illness when she was just 19 months old, which left her deaf, blind and with a significant inability to speak. Imagine for a moment how difficult it can be for a person to start a learning process of any kind without being able to hear or see. Hellen's fortune came when her parents decided to look for an instructor and that is how she met a young

195

and enthusiastic girl named Anne Sullivan. Hellen, years later, despite her physical disability, became the first deaf-blind person to obtain a university degree. Keller is remembered as a prominent activist and philanthropist who promoted women's suffrage and fought for the rights of people with disabilities. For her achievements, the American president Lyndon Johnson gave her the Presidential Medal of the Freedom in 1964, and in 1980, Jimmy Carter, declared the day of her birth as Helen Keller Day.

Questions for your own reflection

1. Do you take care of your body?

2. Do you do it consciously?

3. From 1 to 10, what importance do you give to your body?

4. Did you go through any extreme situation in relation to your health?

5. Do you carry out routine checks periodically?

6. Who comes first, you, your children, your parents, partner, work?

7. Do you cultivate healthy habits (diet, exercise, rest)?

8. Do you correctly establish priorities between health, family and career?

9. Have you ever considered that some characteristic of your body could limit your possibilities?

KNOWLEDGE SKILLS

"Investing in knowledge always produces the best benefits."
Benjamin Franklin

"Our knowledge is necessarily finite, while our ignorance is necessarily infinite."
Karl Popper

What do we understand by knowledge? It is the faculty of the human being to understand the nature, qualities and relationships of things through reason.

9. COGNITION

Cognition is usually understood as the knowledge acquired by a person through experience or education, the theoretical or practical understanding of a matter relating to reality. What is acquired as intellectual content related to a specific field or the entire universe.

Personally, I am convinced that competitiveness demands new ways of doing, whatever we do, whether it is providing a service, assembling a product, carrying out a process, and it is precisely these new ways of doing that require new knowledge and new ways of thinking.

And something that I am passionate about is knowledge management, one of the latest tools in the field of management, which, if we think about it, is nothing more than a new label for a concept as old as humanity itself: ability to learn.

Companies face increasingly volatile, uncertain, complex, ambiguous and demanding environments, with great uncertainty and competitiveness. Under these conditions, only organizations best prepared for innovation, the ability to learn, and the flexibility to adapt and continuously improve can survive.

No technology alone offers a sustainable competitive advantage. If we analyze it, companies have the possibility of acquiring machinery, systems, and technologies; however, they cannot buy talented people committed to organizational values and goals.

We can conclude then that the main factor of competitiveness of organizations has become their knowledge, and the knowledge of the organization is nothing more than that of the people who develop in it, and it is precisely in that knowledge where lies the ability to identify and develop new business opportunities, provide better services, offer new and better products, faster and achieving a lower cost. To achieve this, it is necessary to ensure that people have the necessary information and knowledge and are motivated and trained to face the challenges.

Knowledge allows you to optimize all the

resources of an organization, including the most important resource: the talent of people. Currently, one of the keys for a company to achieve the desired success is to achieve the mobilization of the talent, energy and motivation of its staff, this is what we call: knowledge management.

Today no one questions that people are the main asset of any company, but when we do, we are referring to people who have the knowledge that allows us to add value to the organization.

Personally, especially in this chapter, I have the example of my parents, Luis and Irma, who always instilled in me the study and development of knowledge, as the greatest and most important inheritance that I could receive from them. And that's how the ambition for knowledge and my development made me follow that path that led me to study many things. As a child I was the one who chose the most varied extracurricular activities, such as writing workshops, music, guitar, piano, acting, and after finishing high school, I began a career in architecture, among other workshops that helped in my work activity, which I started a few months before I turned 18.

It was in that work activity, a bit of a secretary, a bit of an administration and a bit of a treasurer, where I was tempted to change my degree and thus, I entered the University of Economic Sciences, where I studied both a degree in Public Accounting and a bachelor's degree in business administration.

At graduation I was distinguished as a standard bearer and a gold medal for the best grades in the last 3 graduate collations. And it was only at that moment that I understood that the goal was within me, as much as it can be in front of you! But don't think that I have a higher coefficient or that I am a supernatural being, I think it is important to clarify this since many times I am wrongly stigmatized in that place, and really the only thing that leads me to improve myself day by day is desire and ambition, yes! The ambition! That word to which we are accustomed to giving a negative connotation, but on which I want to stop for a moment since it is important to clarify its meaning and importance.

Ambition is the intense desire of the individual to achieve the goals he or she sets. Although it is often confused with a desire almost always

204

reserved for material wealth, power and recognition or fame; The word can also acquire a positive connotation and thus ambition can be understood as the desire to stand out above others with constant personal improvement.

It's about setting goals and continually working to meet them. A person with ambitious goals is then one who not only has an established goal or objective, but also has the necessary level of motivation and confidence, the essential energy and sufficient perseverance to achieve it.

In this sense, a person's level of ambition can be decisive when it comes to seeing how far they will go in life. While a person without much ambition can easily settle for what they already have, simply because they do not feel an intense desire to obtain more or be better, an ambitious person can set complicated goals or very long-term goals and is capable of being patient and give everything necessary to achieve it. It is that flame of ambition that makes us more likely to be better students, move up the job hierarchy or obtain a better income, to name a few valid reasons.

And this is how I move through life, convinced

that a person becomes extraordinary simply by doing something "extra" to the ordinary, as simple as that! And, furthermore, if that extra thing that you add is within your heart and your desires, there will always be a place where you can go to look for additional energy.

But returning to the moment of my graduation, a moment etched in my memory, impossible to forget... I ran to the theater where the diplomas were being awarded, I remember that I had only gotten to do my hair in the morning and then I faced a hectic workday which only allowed me to change in the studio and run to the graduation. I enter in a hurry and panting, I ask where I should register, and when I say my last name, the staff begins to comment excitedly: the flag bearer has arrived! The flag bearer has arrived! (They were worried because it was time to start, and I had not arrived or reported my absence). They began to come out from all sides, one grabbed my purse, another put on my sash, they explained the ritual of the ceremony to me and inside I could only think of two things. On the one hand, my parents' excitement at surprising them when I entered the premises, and on the other, I wondered, how did I

206

come to be in this place?

At that precise moment, while all this was happening like in a movie, and I was hidden behind the curtains listening to the opening of the event, waiting for them to announce the entry of the ceremonial flag, I realized that I was there not because I wanted it or for seeking the recognition of the flag or the average, but for having completed the university degree with the goal of learning more. That desire had led me to not fail any exam, to take each class not as jumping an obstacle, and I did not prepare each instance of evaluation to pass an exam, but my attitude and only goal was always to acquire knowledge. My goal was to learn, during these and all careers, postgraduate degrees, master's degrees, courses, projects; My goal is always the same, to learn, to learn content, to learn from practice, to learn from others and with others, and that was what led me to obtain different recognitions, as in this case, not only from institutions but also from people.

I close my eyes and I can feel how my eyes were surprised to see my friends standing, applauding, whistling and shouting my name, good job Marisa!

You are a genius, Marisa! You did it! You deserve it! My professors, who hugged me tight and told me how proud they were that I was the one receiving the recognition, because they remembered me in their class's chairs.

Also, my business partner, Doctor Héctor Francisco Valcarce, who at that time was Treasurer of the Professional Council of Economic Sciences Avellaneda Delegation, who strutted around with the president of the Lomas de Zamora Delegation Council, simply because she was his employee at that time.

And what can I tell you about my parents, their emotion and pride was so great, so, so great! Despite never having required me to achieve a certain grade, there was something about the values and advice they had taught me that had generated meaning in the way I approached life.

And so, I continued my development, my career, my life, and of course always pragmatic, I put the acquired knowledge into practice, since I definitely consider that experience generates a fundamental contribution in the virtuous circle of knowledge.

208

Important tips

Now I would like to share some important tips to optimize our practice of learning and expand our knowledge, both personally and in the organizations in which we work.

- ✓ Be willing to share knowledge.

- ✓ Question any premise and recognize what is unknown.

- ✓ Develop learning in a climate of trust and transparency.

- ✓ Cancel fears of failing, losing or making mistakes.

- ✓ Provide information to others so that they can generate contributions to the organization or benefit themselves.

- ✓ Generate awareness of a common shared destiny, which facilitates coordination and teamwork. Everyone rowing in the same boat and in the same direction, everyone's success depends on the ability of the team and not on individual capabilities.

- ✓ Combine the aptitude that knowledge provides with the appropriate attitude, because the

209

application of knowledge depends on people's motivation. If the people who have the knowledge are not committed, they will not put it into practice.

✓ Lead by example of stated values.

✓ Develop a leadership style based on knowledge and values.

✓ Generate mechanisms where people realize the opportunity to fulfill themselves personally at work, feeling respected and valued for what they do.

✓ Make decisions by consensus, avoiding the imposition of arbitrary hierarchical power.

✓ Recognize and reward people for their performance and their ability to add value to the organization and not for their seniority, status or obedience to arbitrarily imposed rules. People are not in organizations just to do their jobs but to add value.

Personal story: Knowledge makes a difference

There is a time when analysis, reasoning and good decision making count when it comes to

210

achieving excellent performance, that is why in this chapter I want to bring you an anecdote where I had to carry out an important intervention by AFIP to the company, in relation to compliance with Decree 814/01, completely interpretive, where being categorized in subsection a or b generated a distance that translated into a few million dollars of difference.

In mid-2004 we received a request from the tax agency, requesting a large amount of information and documentation to comply within a peremptory period of 14 days. When the date arrives, the officials are attended to by the *Controller* of the company and after spending several days validating data, they notify us of the opening of the intervention to the company, for which they request a venue, office or meeting room, since the process takes a significant time, where the officials settle to carry out its inspection task.

The company was extremely neat, carried out all the processes that were legally imposed and paid the corresponding taxes imposed by national, provincial and municipal organizations.

Now, without wanting to bore you in a tax

aspect, I will briefly explain the claim generated by the treasury in relation to Decree 814/01, where it established a benefit of 4 percentage points of reduction in the cost of social charges on the payroll to companies that were either categorized as SMEs (respecting certain parameters) when they involved service or trade activities, or when the company's main business was industrial activities. The company that had applied said benefit, for several years, from the publication of the aforementioned decree, until the moment of the intervention, because it considered media activity as an industry, had to face the defense of a claim that amounted to almost 2 million dollars, and it was my knowledge that gave me great help on this issue, I knew I had to defend my position, and I knew where to go.

While many were concerned about finding a way not to exceed the parameters as services, I was convinced that what did not give rise to any refutation was considering the activity as an industry. There were long-standing norms that categorized it as such, even the President of the Nation herself in a speech (which I especially sought to present as another element of defense) referred to the "highly valued media industry." So, I brought together a great team made up of several accountants, tax specialists, tax lawyers and administrators, to wage a battle not only with a great economic impact for the organization, but also to show legal security for our country towards American shareholders and ethics regarding decision-making that was timely implemented and continued to be respected to this day. The process takes several years, and what I can tell you at the time of writing this book is that the first three administrative and judicial instances validated the company's position. Although the Supreme Court has not yet ruled on the underlying issue, all sources validate the interpretation adopted and justify the application of section b of the famous Decree 814/01.

Grace Murray Hopper

In this chapter I want to remember the great Grace Murray Hopper, a pioneer in computer science. Currently it is difficult to imagine our daily lives without computers, whether at work or at home, to talk with friends, to watch shows or to shop online, the computer is essential and essential in our homes.

And precisely to whom we owe a lot for this is Grace, a pioneer in the world of technology and programming language, since today her scientific legacy becomes even more relevant. This New York woman studied mathematics and physics and reached the rank of rear admiral in the armed forces. She invented the first compiler, a software that was responsible for translating a programming language into a language that was understood by a machine and could be processed. Her advances were important in developing the first modern programming languages.

Finally, I share with you one of her wonderfully inspiring quotes: "A ship in port is safe, but that is not what ships are built for. Sail on the sea and do new things."

Questions for your own reflection

1. *Did you dream of studying something that seemed difficult to you?*

2. *How do you think a learning-oriented culture is promoted?*

3. *Have you ever found that it was too late to start studying something new?*

4. *What internal difficulties do you feel that do not allow you to promote innovation that favors learning?*

5. *Are you trying to learn about what happens to you as a person, as a team or as a family?*

6. *Are you looking to find sources of knowledge for factual knowledge?*

7. *Is the classroom a place to learn or reflect on what happens to us?*

8. *Do you think that diversity influences the richness of knowledge?*

10. COMMUNICATION

"Wise men speak because they have something to say; fools because they have to say something."

Plato

"Whatever words we use, they should be used carefully because the people who hear them will be influenced for better or worse."

Buddha

All companies report having communication problems, all leaders acknowledge failing in many objectives because of this reason, communication problems are mentioned in all teams that do not allow them to advance in projects.

"Major changes are generally impossible unless the majority of employees are willing to help to the point of making short-term sacrifices. But people won't make those sacrifices, even if they're unhappy with the current situation, unless they think the potential benefits of change are attractive and unless they think true transformation is possible. Without frequent and credible communication, the hearts of employees will never be captured."

John P. Kotter Autor de Leading Change

That said, there is no doubt that one of the main skills of a good leader is being able to communicate and influence people. Without communication, there are no followers, so there can hardly be any leadership. The motivation of work teams depends enormously on the communication that the leader has with them, for this reason I consider that this capacity is one of the fundamental ones to become good leaders.

Communication is an absolutely powerful tool, it has the ability to create, strengthen, improve relationships when used well, but be careful! Because, just as it can help us, it also becomes a negative tool when it is not properly managed, generating the opposite effect, destroying labor, commercial, corporate and all kinds of relationships.

It's a skill to work on, it's that simple! That is why I'm inviting you to develop good assertive communication.

I want to stop for a moment, since it is no less important to be able to identify the predominant communication style in each of us, considering that we can distinguish the passive, the aggressive and the assertive.

The passive is characterized by not saying what they really want and need to say. These types of people are those who permanently avoid conflict, we usually call them "those who have a weak yes". Although we can point out the good level of listening as an advantage, the disadvantage is outweighed in the negative aspect since they fail to realize their interests, in addition to ending up exploding or imploding when they react to some abuses to which the interlocutor themselves agreed.

The aggressive, almost the opposite pole of the passive, is the communicator with verbosity who does not stop to listen, who says everything they wants to say, without paying attention to the other and without a filter, whom we commonly call "without mincing words.". This style, totally lacking in empathy, has the advantage that they manage to say what they want, but its negative is the absence or low level of listening.

Assertive is the ideal and recommended communication style, since they communicate what they want, but doing so in a firm and respectful manner, putting themselves in the other's shoes. Therefore, this style of communication allows for the development of lasting bonds and turns out to be absolutely effective.

Due to which, the recommendation is to work on this last communication style. But when doing it, it shouldn't be any way, the key is to be accurate, when you are accurate it works, otherwise it doesn't. Being accurate and well informed is a requirement for all types of communication. The lack of depth and certainty, in addition to not producing the desired result, generates a counterproductive effect in every possible sense.

If we delve into its meaning, certainty comes from certain, it is the sure and clear knowledge of something, it is the firm adherence of the mind to something known, without fear of error. The latter seems fundamental and very important to me to highlight, "to not be afraid to make mistakes", it is always possible to change something, it is always possible to improve and make something more perfect. I would say that it is even acceptable to be alert, but it should only work that way and not as a barrier, since in general women are often afraid of making mistakes and that single thought is like an attraction to failing. For this reason, I want to recommend that you seek to be prudent because that makes you effective people and professionals, but be careful with the excesses, that can lead you to become fearful people, and that position definitely does not add up.

Now, despite the importance of developing an assertive communication style, we must not lose sight of the fact that according to neurolinguistic programming, the meaning that a person assigns to what is said or communicated to them is made up of only 7 % for what has been said, while the vocal component (tone, volume) is assigned 38%, and the corporal component (posture, corporality) is assigned the remaining 55%. This means that it is not enough to prepare the content of the message, the way in which we express ourselves physically and the tone of voice we use is also very important and has a greater impact on the result. These three well-articulated aspects make us good, average or bad communicators.

Nor should we overlook the difference that exists between informing and communicating,

220

since when I inform, I emit a message, but when I communicate, I must make sure what the message is interpreted by the person who receives it, since communication is constituted both by what I emit and by what the other interprets from my message. Therefore, it is extremely important and differential for a leader to adjust the message to the audience and validate it with them.

And here I want to share with you the importance of identifying the audience to whom you are addressing, to whom you are communicating. A leader who knows how to communicate assertively has the ability to differentiate the preferred communication styles of his audience. Among the most relevant and returning to NLP, are the auditory, visual and kinesthetic ones. Being able to differentiate them allows you to select the most appropriate means of communication for each of them. If the person you lead is auditory, your means of communication should be face to face or even by telephone or voice audio, but don't expect them to understand everything you convey in writing. On the contrary, a visual person needs to "read you," and requires that you put emphasis on written messages by

221

email, presentations or documents. In the case of kinesthetics, they are people who prioritize the experience, assimilate the messages by watching you act, accompanying your message through the practice of a specific action or a story that you tell them and that exemplifies what you are trying to convey to them. When you know your team, you can observe them and quickly identify, through the words they use, what communication or learning modality they prefer. The visual ones speak faster and use verbs like "I see", "I visualize"; The auditory ones express themselves at a medium speed with verbs such as "it resonates with me", "what I hear" and the kinesthetic ones use a slower speed to express themselves and speak both in terms of action such as "put it into practice" and linked to emotions and feelings "what I feel", "what I identify with".

Finally, let me point out the close relationship that exists between communication and emotions. Therefore, let's accept that when we are angry, we communicate poorly! That's why the last recommendation I make is to count to 10 before responding in a face-to-face dialogue, leave an email that is difficult to answer in draft, and think and rehearse a difficult conversation to maintain, since with more balanced emotions one can act more effectively and this contributes to the assertiveness of communication.

In this chapter, I bring you two anecdotes.

Personal Story: Listen beyond what employees communicate

This first one happened in 2008. The media company where I worked as SVP HR, had established as one of its goals to measure the work environment in all the operations established on the different continents, and for this it was decided to implement the methodology of *Great Place to Work*, which in addition to having a good standard for climate measurement, allowed international analysis to be carried out, and added to a work carried out by many operations in different parts of the world that had already been applying this tool.

After doing a great job with the consultants who accompanied the implementation, we received the results with a depth of analysis that allowed us to evaluate and test possible actions with a great level of detail.

This is how we worked on the development and implementation of an internal communication strategy, together with the great professional and current friend Alejandra Brandolini, president of AB COM, among many other roles that she plays with such expertise.

The work carried out was wonderful, both in terms of results and as a professional and personal experience. We carried out a prior audit, a process that was carried out with extreme care and level of detail. The information collected allowed us to adjust both the internal communication policy, as well as the channels, messages and spokespersons, but in the middle of the analysis an incredible finding arose: employees were complaining about the benefits that the company provided them! And I can't explain to you the budget that was invested in that item and the number of benefits they received! From health, insurance, gifts on special dates such as the end of the year, Father's and Mother's Day, Children's Day, start of school, celebration of important dates such as Easter, special training, language training, gym, and a long list of many more benefits.

224

The budget that was invested was a significant percentage of the total *payroll* and the employees complained about what they received! It was unbelievable! The surveys were anonymous, but I remember dedicating an entire weekend to reading conclusions and details and, in each comment, I thought I heard the employee who was saying it (at that time a company with almost 600 total payroll employees).

The following week, while I was working with the team and we couldn't get over the shock and indignation, EUREKA! We began to sharpen the analysis and break down the data and we came to the conclusion that the people who did not value the health plan were the young employees, the older one were not interested in the gym, the single employees did not value the life insurance but claimed *work-life balance (defined by the Cambridge dictionary as the time one spends at work compared to the time spent with family and activities one enjoys)*. And so on I can mention a long list, so I called the team together and we got to work on an innovative *Flexible Benefit Plan*, which consisted of a system of credits, which were granted according to the level of the position, aligned to the compensation

225

structure, whose main characteristics were: that the employee was the one who could annually put together their benefits plan, assigning the credits received according to the personal preference of their tastes and needs. Another requirement was not to exceed the invested budget and finally it had to be easy to manage administratively for the employee and for the human resources department.

This is how this absolutely new plan for the time generated a very important impact on the climate, level of satisfaction and *engagement* of the employees. It was also awarded locally by Meta 4, as the HR Innovation Award, and internationally by the *board* of HR by innovative practice. We worked helping to replicate it in other operations and in other companies in Argentina, and it was all thanks to being able to communicate properly with our employees.

Personal Story: Communicating beyond language barriers

In this chapter I wanted to bring a second anecdote, to show the effect of barriers on communication.

226

We were at the first board meeting that the CEO for LATAM had called in Miami. It is worth clarifying that at that point I had an advanced level of English, but I interacted with native and bilingual speakers of the language. For this reason, even though on the streets of Miami everyone speaks more Spanish than the American language, in the company, since one of the directors was a native English speaker and did not know Spanish, communications were mostly in English.

We were almost at the end of the meeting, and the last item on the agenda consisted of defining the purchase of a niche sports channel. For which we had to analyze the indicators presented by our boss, CEO of LATAM, and vote, in order to express our decision in this regard. The investment was important, more than 1.5 million dollars, which is why, given the confusion about the type of valuation of said company, I request that they repeat the aforementioned ratios and then expand on the valuation criteria.

At that moment, the CFO, a Spaniard with an aggressive communication style, raising his tone of voice quite a bit, tells me: *"Excuse me Marisa, are you*

227

not fully bilingual? Honestly, we are all senior executives (the board was made up of 7 male directors and me) and our time is extremely valuable, we can't be interrupting just because you don't understand".

These are the occasions where counting to 3.5 or 10 helps a lot and allows us to make a difference and carry out assertive communication. So, remembering this I breathed, I breathed again, and with great height I responded: *"You are right, I am not bilingual, but I can communicate without any difficulties. Obviously, when the shareholders offered me to take the position of director of operations and be part of this board, they did it knowing that I was not bilingual and trusting in my abilities for such a responsible position and it is precisely that responsibility for such an important decision which leads me to make sure of my understanding."*

Although it is currently mandatory to speak English, it was not at the time of my hiring to the company and when they offered me the COO position, they evidently took more into account the skills I have as a leader than my level of English.

But you know what? The most important thing was my breathing, my tone of voice, my corporality, my intonation and my gaze... the security of my message was reflected in my entire being and with respect, I made his misguided intervention evident; Of course, one of the many unpleasant situations that I had to experience during my corporate career and one of the reasons that prompted me to write this book for you. So that you can leave with some learning and tools that help you navigate your professional path better.

Hedy Lamarr

As the woman chosen to honor this chapter, I bring the beautiful Hedy Lamarr, who in addition to being an actress, reigned in the Olympus of golden Hollywood. She had an admirable glamour, which balances her other, more unknown facets. The artist was not only a sex symbol, but she was the owner of a privileged mind and the author of a communications system on which all existing technologies today are based. You could say that it is the precursor of the current WIFI.

Inventing was her true passion. Her favorite subject was chemistry and from an early age she began to be interested in technology, just like her father, whom she adored. She developed a parallel and quite discreet career as telecommunications engineer and helped magnate Howard Hughes in his obsession with creating a faster airplane, studying the aerodynamics of birds and the physiognomy of fish.

And before saying goodbye to the exciting topic of communication, I leave you to reflect on your predominant communication style.

Questions for your own reflection

1. How do you identify your communication style? Are you passive, aggressive or assertive?

2. Are you accurate? Do you handle yourself with certainty?

3. How do emotions affect you when you communicate?

4. Do you tend to assume interpretations in messages?

5. Do you have communication barriers that prevent you from being effective with the message?

6. What is your listening level?

7. Do you generally inform or communicate? Do you take care of checking the interpretation of the message?

8. Think about your first high-exposure, high-impact presentation. How did you prepare?

11.CRITERION

"I like people with judgment, those who are not ashamed to admit that they don't know something or that they were wrong."

Mario Benedetti

"You have to love what is worthy of being loved and hate what is hateful, but good judgment is needed to distinguish between the one and the other."

Robert Lee Frost

On many occasions speaking with colleagues, we have mentioned the importance of having judgment in our collaborators, peers, leaders and even in ourselves.

That's why before getting into the topic I would like to start by clarifying the concept. When we talk about criteria, what do we mean?

The term criterion has its origin in a Greek word κριτήριον (kritérion), which in turn derives from the verb κρίνειν (krínein), meaning "to judge". A criterion is the principle or norm according to which the truth can be known, a determination can be made, or an opinion or judgment can be made on a particular matter.

The meaning of criterion is judgment or the ability of people to make a judgment about something or someone according to the information they have. It means the opinion about something.

In this sense, criteria is what allows us to establish the guidelines or principles from which we can distinguish one thing from the other, such as what is true from what is false, what is correct from what is incorrect, what makes sense from what doesn't.

Thus, the criterion is associated with the rational faculty of the human being to make decisions and make judgments, which is why it is a fundamental tool to establish differences and make decisions, whether they are correct or not, depending on the sources that we take advantage of to enrich our criteria.

The fact that it is formed from our diverse experiences and sources that enrich and influence it, to a greater or lesser extent, makes the criterion have a subjective nature, the basis of constructivism, which explains that a person will understand something in one way or another depending on their past experiences, their history, their way of seeing life, etc.

We say that speaking with judgment is speaking knowing what is being said. Hence, criterion also refers to the capacity of a person to make a judgment, adopt an opinion or make a resolution on some issue: "I do not have criteria to give an opinion on matters of Byzantine art, since I know nothing about the subject."

In this way, criteria can also be used as a synonym for judgment or discernment: "Paul prefers to always incorporate vegetables into his meals, because, according to his criteria, it is healthier to be a vegetarian."

Criterion is essential when making decisions, making evaluations or expressing our point of view regarding something. In this sense, the criterion is not only applied in all disciplines of knowledge, but also in the most diverse facets of life.

Good judgment is essential in leadership. A leader is judged by the results and performance of their organization, these results depend largely on the decisions the leader makes. Success will depend not only on the decision made and the moment in which it is made, but also on the result that it produces and that will have a lot to do with how the leader manages the decision-making process as a whole and its implementation.

I remember as if it were today a dialogue with my 6-year-old daughter, when after helping her with the explanation of one of her first school assignments, she raised her little head, directed her gaze directly toward mine and with those divine eyes of admiration, with her serious tone of voice and accompanying the expression of her gaze, she tells me:

—Mommy, you know everything!

I smiled and told her that that was her perception, but that I was simply sharing something from a lot of knowledge that I acquired like her at her age, but that I definitely didn't know everything.

—Mommy, how can one know everything? — she continued asking and after a moment she exclaimed—When I grow up, I want to know everything!

That made me think, I was always very curious and ambitious, especially with knowledge, but that goal, that dream had never crossed my mind, much less at that age, but on the contrary, growing up, I was trained, I acquired various formal education and I faced many authors, teachers, professors, instructors, businessmen, with different opinions that I shared on some occasions and not on others.

But I found that these very respectable people from their knowledge or experiences and life paths, shared their expositions as the absolute truth, and it was at that moment when I understood that I had a criterion, that I could discern from what others maintained, and I could justify with objective capacity the validity of my judgments.

Personal story: The value-based criterion

The anecdote that I will tell you in this chapter is related to the business of the company that I had to manage as General Manager.

Three years ago, we had begun to develop our strategy for the sustainable development of the media business, where we did not stop pursuing the economic goal, but now we had also defined a corporate sustainability matrix that imposed new objectives on us.

Without ceasing to take care of the economic aspect, we also defined goals that achieved the environmental and social impact of our company. Thus, we began to work on aspects that would collaborate in the development of a careful digital society, through the inclusion of older adults in this new world, working on the protection of children and adolescents in their exposure on the networks and investing in the community as a whole in different ways.

We also began to measure and manage the impact that our business generated on the environment, which is why we implemented many actions: taking care of electronic waste disposal, reducing the carbon footprint, making energy consumption more efficient, in addition to donating paper and plastic, which we had begun to coordinate more than eight years ago. In principle with paper and since 2006 we added the plastic lids, together with the Dr. Juan P. Garrahan Hospital, who have a program that involves the entire society in relation to these donations and is then assembled with a voluntary logistics chain which ends in the delivery of large volumes of material to recycling companies. In this field we also organize annual plantations with the aim of compensating for the minimum consumption that we could not avoid carrying out the business.

We work inside the organization, with our employees, in corporate management and the value chain with our clients and suppliers. To our clients, we offered information privacy, guaranteeing data security and providing innovation in quality services and products. All this as something absolutely innovative at that time. Both clients and suppliers were also offered the possibility of joining and replicating any of our programs, collaborating in their implementation.

Although I am not going to stop by recounting all the management implemented based on the defined strategy, in relation to customer care and the excellence of the product provided, a strategic alliance was made with the Cibersegura Foundation. We developed a protection campaign that we called #quelarednoteenrede, (don't get trapped on the trap) which consisted of animated shorts with the participation of the figures on our screen, where we addressed topics such as

238

cyberbullying, grooming and reputation *on line,* to cycles of wonderful documentaries on the topic of gender violence: "Women who do not shut up" and "When I said enough", a topic that was comprehensively addressed and accompanied by the generation of bills that seek to generate changes that help to remedy the problem.

But now yes! Getting into the topic of this chapter, I tell you that the programming of the channels was in charge of the Content Director, with the supervision of a Programming Committee that had my final approval, which in general did not offer changes, since it had a team of superb professionals who did their job wonderfully, but on this occasion a case arose that merited my judgment and that I bring to you to illustrate the ability that I think is so important in a leader.

Material had been purchased for the Europa signal - one of the channels in our portfolio and whose essence was to program exquisite European material from period films, contemporary films, series and documentaries - among the acquisitions was a series that showed the violent treatment of an Italian woman. It was an absolute box office hit and promised great ratings, which generated high traditional advertising rates, as well as sponsorships that translated into excellent income for the company. The Committee never raises the point and only reports its title in the following month's schedule with a simple description of the argument and an observation. Upon noticing this, I requested the background information and, despite having a lot of resistance from the content director and the entire Committee due to the economic results that said title promised, my criteria led me to remove the series from the screen. And what lead me to make the decision? The economic result of the company could not be in contrast to the social aspect and reflect a lack of coherence between the content that our screen would broadcast, leaving a message to the audience that was totally contradictory to the sustainability strategy—which, among other goals— defended the vulnerability of women and gender violence.

It is very important in every person, but fundamentally in a leader, who in addition to managing, teaches by example to apply and defends their criteria in the battery of decisions they make periodically.

240

Angela Merkel

While in Latin America, rulers respond like leaders to the challenge posed by COVID-19, either imposing curfews or ignoring the threat, in Germany, Chancellor Merkel is governing calmly and peacefully, making decisions with judgment, which is reflected in the polls, since she has great approval from the Germans, who trust their leader when circumstances change dramatically as is happening with this pandemic, and threaten to get out of control, as happened in the overturn of their country's nuclear energy policy after the Fukushima disaster.

As a good physicist, Merkel works based on facts, and leads the pandemic crisis at times when it is impossible to predict its evolution, adapting its management to the factual circumstances that occur moment by moment and the conclusions that her own criteria and that of her advisors determine.

Questions for your own reflection

1. *What is your opinion on criterion?*

2. *Do you used to defend your judgment?*

3. *When you applied your criteria, did you consider it to be assertive?*

4. *What is your rational when you use your judgment?*

5. *Have they ever shown you that your judgment was wrong?*

6. *Do you consider that people are born with criteria or is it formed throughout life?*

7. *Have you trained your judgment?*

12.COHERENCE

"It is easier to fight for principles than live on agreement with them."
Alfred Adler

"The identity of a man consists of the coherence between what he is and what he thinks."
Charles Sandeers Peirce

What are we talking about when we talk about coherence?

When we define the meaning of coherence, we say that it is the cohesion or relationship between one thing and another. The concept is used to name something that is logical and consistent with respect to an antecedent. Coherence is, consequently, something that maintains the same line with a previous position.

Particularly in this chapter, for consistency we refer to the consistent attitude of a person in relation to a previously assumed position. In this sense, when we say that someone is coherent, it is because it is verified that there is a correspondence

243

between their way of thinking, feeling and behaving, the famous *"walk the talk"*.

Now, if leadership is the set of managerial skills that an individual has to influence the way people or a work team act, making them work with enthusiasm to achieve their goals and objectives, then, a coherent leader is one who acts, not based on what is most comfortable or simple, but who thinks before acting about the potential consequences of their actions on other people, teams and systems with which they interact to avoid negative or unwanted impacts.

That is why when this ability is present and we develop leadership that has coherent behavior, we find as a result a comprehensive, honest and authentic process in relation to what we think, feel and do.

In this line of thinking, this leadership must be absolutely consistent between what it demands of its reports and work teams and what the leader contributes to the rest. We also say that you must act by example and in tune with what you think, assuming the consequences derived from it, because only in this way will you achieve the

244

necessary credibility to lead effectively and authentically.

When the leader has authentic behavior and is motivated by positive thoughts and feelings, they say what they believe and believe in what they say, their influence on the team will always be positive. What is also important is that this also works the other way around, when there is no coherence, this negatively influences the team.

In coherence comes a spirit for the common good, it is like the pirinola spinning top option, sorry to the younger ones! I open a parenthesis to tell you that "la pirinola" was a game that consisted of following the instructions of a rotating element and one of the options was "everyone wins" the famous *win-win*. The person, the leader, the team, the other teams, the organization, the shareholder, the supplier, the client, the entire society wins. Now, when this spirit is not present, one is not leading, but rather one is exercising power.

To exercise leadership, efficient management of work teams is required, generating trust among the people who make up them and interact in the organization; seek to convey to each one their important role and impact on the final product or service and the results, and convey a shared vision of the future of the company, aimed at obtaining realistic challenges and goals, achieving common and individual goals at the same time, because harmony must be established between both. Furthermore, and no less important, the leader must promote the autonomy of their members in their actions and taking initiatives.

So, if I have to list the characteristics that a coherent leader must have, I will summarize it in the following:

- A coherent leader first leads themselves as a starting point, since those who are not capable of leading their own life cannot lead other people.

- Not being master of your own life makes you live at the mercy of circumstances. It is very important for the leader to have great knowledge of themselves, to know their values and principles.

- They are aware of their talent, their strengths and their areas of improvement.

246

- And, above all, they know what their leadership and life purpose is.

- They develop trust as a core skill, which allows them to develop a bond that enables them to trust others and for others to trust them as well.

- They are sincere and fulfill their commitments.

- They show balance and serenity in their actions and decisions.

- They have the ability to put focus and attention on what is important.

- They properly manage their emotions and puts them at the service of their purpose.

- They maintain a personal and professional conciliation.

- They are absolutely transparent; they show themselves as they are.

- They are available and empathetic with the way they look at others.

- They develop lasting relationships through example and conversation.

- They do not remain with the function of the

employee, they are interested in the person who functions in the middle of the ecosystem and who is a fundamental gear for its operation, as much as he or the rest of the people and teams that complement each other with other tasks and other areas.

- They are flexible and adapt to context, situations and changes, accepting uncertainty and always valuing opportunity, diversity and difference.

- They have the great virtue of transforming problems into challenges, from which they in turn nourish, learn and motivate.

So why is coherence a fundamental value for developing the role of leader? It is because of this ability that they get the power to strengthen and consolidate a work team, in such a way that all its members feel comfortable with it and thus a solid, long-term relationship is generated, in which trust prevails.

In short, coherence allows theory to be articulated with practice, it is a fundamental element for the leader to be credible, have integrity and encourage the team to act in the same way,

248

since it is precisely this coherence that generates trust in the group, and in return, it is this trust that facilitates communication and influence that allows the achievement of common results.

Why should leaders be consistent? Because leadership is a responsibility in which the leader must prioritize collective interests over their own personal interests. In particular, you must lead according to the mission, vision and values of the organization, and in order to do so consistently, you must ensure that you exercise your leadership role in a company or organization that shares your values.

Now, since this choice is often not made considering these aspects, but rather when choosing which company to work for, managers choose work projects based on other aspects, what ends up happening is that this lack of coherence makes them, in the best case, good managers, but mediocre leaders and this is how, in the absence of harmony between purposes and values, they end up not leading but rather exercising power, two completely different things!

Personal stories: I speak from my own example

Therefore, in relation to this important characteristic of coherence, I chose two situations to share with you among the many that I have had, where coherence is evident in my actions and decisions, by my way of thinking, feeling and acting.

The first situation took place in 2008, due to a crisis that I had to manage where the world's economies were hit by the bankruptcy of the fourth largest investment bank in the United States, *Lehman Brothers*, a fall that, together with that of other institutions, would bring important consequences for the global financial system, which added to the collapse of the real estate bubble that began two years earlier, which began to manifest itself dramatically at the beginning of that year, impacting first on the US financial system, and then internationally.

Additionally, the high prices of commodities collapsed, and the countries that supplied food and energy to the global economic system saw their income drastically reduced.

To the decrease in income resulting from the international fall in the price of raw materials, the drop caused by lower demand of them added up, a perfect combo for the vulnerable situation of our country.

Of course, the company I led, despite being economically and financially healthy, suffered the impact of the contraction of the Latin American markets where we developed our business, and in order to achieve the margin of *EBITDA* that we had committed ourselves to the shareholders in the *Budget* approved for that year. In October we had to implement an adjustment of some cost lines that did not directly impact the business, but that at the same time have a significant specific weight. Therefore, from the analysis it turned out that we had to cut the amount assigned to the item of *Travel & Expenses*, used, as most of you know, for airfare, lodging and meal expenses on business trips.

This is how we stopped complying with the established policy, which was temporarily suspended, until the economy began to give in to its crisis and the business was able to accommodate itself.

Although it is true that by making the times more efficient for those of us who were traveling and had a hectic schedule, flights were generally coordinated at night (especially for those of us who were based in South America, where moving almost anywhere in the world meant more than 6 hours of flight) which allowed me to be producing first thing in the office in another city, whether attending a meeting, closing a contract or carrying out an important negotiation. But to be lucid and have enough energy to achieve good performance, it is advisable to fly in Business, which allows our body and mind to rest as much and as well as possible.

The policy of *T&E (Travel & Expenses)* of the company, provided for different categories of tickets considering basically two situations: the kilometers traveled and the seniority of the person making the trip. However, there were exceptions, such as health situations or the purpose of the trip that may contemplate category changes. But this economic situation forced us to lower the travel categories, where the difference in prices between Business and Economy were important. I mention this because when making costs more efficient, you must always be very careful not to make ineffective and unpleasant decisions such as changing the coffee brand, which causes more losses than one can imagine. But this was not the situation, so the tickets were reduced to *Economy* in all cases and depending on the flight distances and the agreement with each employee, the arrival at the destination was scheduled one day in advance to be able to stay one night in a hotel before starting the work that had led them to travel abroad.

The changes in travel policies mainly affect the sales areas and the CEO, who are the ones who travel most frequently, although there are trips by other executives such as CFO, COO, SVP HR and SVP Legal, in general the companies that make these types of decisions exempts the first line, leaving only the rest of the employees affected by the adjustment.

But on this occasion, I was the one who was leading the company and I did not feel comfortable with the decision to exclude the first line of executives or exclude myself (as the shareholders had suggested) since it did not seem coherent to implement this rule that affected all employees,

253

while I continued traveling in First or Business, for the simple reason that we all run the company together and we all perform different, but no less important, functions.

For this reason, I acted in two ways, on the one hand I gathered the directors and informed them of my decision, the majority agreed, one of the directors apologized for her age and I received another attempt to resist which I did not accept, telling him that if he did not agree with the measure, he could either replace his place of travel with someone from his team or contribute his miles to upgrade to the category he desired (generated by his own frequent traveler activity).

I also instructed my secretary that the travel arrangements of all employees, without exception, were carried out in Economy until the company improved its finances.

For that reason, for more than 2 years, I traveled in Economy, and I argued with more than one director of the company who demanded preferential treatment, giving in on some occasions to the director who, because of her age, had a health problem that prevented her from traveling under certain conditions.

This simple decision that demonstrates our coherence between what we say and what we do as managers, setting an example, has more impact on people, teams and companies than many other awards or marketing actions that have an immediate effect, but that are ephemeral and short-term.

The second situation that I remembered when writing this book was when I suddenly found a photograph on the computer, where we were, together with a group of volunteers, traveling to the school sponsored by the company, based on incorporating the company's strategy of sustainable media business, where the business model is crossed by the concept of *Triple Bottom Line* by which it stops measuring only the economic results of the company, but also incorporates the impact of its activity on the environment and society.

Convinced from my core that the future of companies must be 100% sustainable, I began to investigate, I began to introduce sustainable practices that collaborated in an invisible way to change habits, leading to cultural transformation over time. So I took care of implementing practices that would help with the carbon footprint, I looked carefully at the content that was broadcast on our screens, making sure that it did not disrupt our values, we worked on programs that would take care of employees, allowing their development and satisfaction in their workplaces and many more actions that led us to become one of the first companies in the media industry to implement a comprehensive sustainable strategy.

And in this journey of doing it silently, we developed a corporate volunteer program, of which I was a part of as any other member. In that space we carried out different activities, for example we organized annual plantations that I attended with my daughter, and we gave ourselves the luxury of sweating while planting trees.

We also sponsored a school in Calabacilla, Entre Ríos, which we helped from its conditioning, kitchen, library, computer room and garden, to supplies, clothing and food for the students who, with great sacrifice and enthusiasm, attended daily.

To do this, we carried out collections among the staff, we looked for sponsors to collaborate with necessary products, we prepared activities to carry out with the children and we organized two or three annual trips, where a group of volunteers traveled in the company van.

We worked preparing materials, cooking delicious things for the kids who were waiting for us with a huge smile, and the employees who shared a different closeness by working side by side with me, were amazed and told me that it had never happened to them and they had never heard of cases in which the CEO of the company became directly involved with issues that were not the exclusive responsibility of its function.

Honestly, that was consistency on display in all its glory, doing exactly what I think and feel, what I invite others to feel and do. Of course, this type of situation generates a bond of trust in the people we lead, which is not comparable with any other action we can take.

Virginia Wolff

A woman who seems to me to be a tribute to coherence by excellence is Virginia Wolff, who suffered several depressions throughout her life, and her first was at the age of 13 with the death of her mother. In the following years, she was also a victim of sexual abuse by her stepbrothers, creating within her a strong mentality of fighting against sexism that she reflected in her work. Virginia Wolff was a British writer who, with her novels and writings, became one of the greatest symbols of feminism and literary modernism of the 20th century. In fact, her essay "A Room of One's Own," dating from 1923, is one of the most cited texts by the movement.

Questions for your own reflection

1. *Do you value consistency? How much from 1 to 10?*

2. *Do you consider yourself a coherent person?*

3. *If there is an income and expense policy, do you record your company income and expenses?*

4. *Do you only drink if your assistant brings it to you or do you pour yourself coffee without a problem when you feel like it?*

5. *Do you participate in solidarity campaigns? Such as? Running the marathon or organizing everything with your team?*

6. *Do you defend decisions, which may be unpleasant, if you are convinced that they are correct?*

7. *In a crisis, do you take the helm or take refuge in the bow?*

8. *Do you demand from others things that you don't like to do?*

PART THREE

GET INTO ACTION!

If you really want to do something, if you believe in it... just keep going, and success will follow.

Cassandra Sanford, Grupo Kelly Mitchell

Many women live as if they were in a dress rehearsal. Ladies, the curtain is up, and you are on the stage.

Mikki Taylor, editor of Essence magazine

Women in the field of work

Women do not naturally occupy leadership positions, in fact, in recent decades, there has been progress in the participation of women in the professional, business and organization fields in general, and this is how the number of women grew in the different endowments. But these places are represented by the base of the organizational pyramid, and are sometimes reserved for certain areas, but they hardly occupy a decision-making position, and there are few cases of women leading companies as number one.

However, diversity is represented by the formation of a parity that results from the balanced participation of women and men in decision-making positions in both the economic, political and social areas.

I am convinced, like many others, that women must deploy their talent in organizations and be able to occupy the positions they want, without having to deal with situations such as glass ceilings

263

or any other prejudice.

According to the *Global Gender Gap Report 2016* produced by the World Economic Forum, parity would be achieved in approximately 165 years. The majority of women are concerned about accessing decision-making positions in organizations, mainly due to the level of time commitment, and also, in my opinion, because they assign more importance to cultural or organizational barriers than to personal ones.

Additionally, one of the main reasons that stops the development of women in decision-making positions, that is, if they are outside the agreement, is salary, which does not happen when the functions are conventional, where the norm is equal to both sexes. Women in this segment earn on average half as much as men for the same work and with the same level of responsibilities and training. Even though, in most cases, women work longer hours.

In Argentina the average gap is 25%[3] and to that we must add the impact of unpaid work, such as

---

[3] Fuente Global Wage Report 2018/19

264

care tasks, which further expands this gap.

Another problem is female participation in the total labor force, since only 58% manage to work while for men this ratio reaches 79%.[4] While the employment rate is 21 pp (percentage points) lower in women than in men in the labor market in general, there are 3 sectors such as: teaching, health and domestic service where women are the ones with the highest participation. But when we look at the unemployment rates, understood as the percentage that represents the number of people without work in relation to the economically active population looking for work, women are 1.9 pp above men.[5]

But what is most significant are the ratios related to the number of women occupying the highest positions in organizations, which continues to be at very low levels in general terms. While only 37% of management positions are occupied by women, this percentage drops to 15% in director and executive positions, and only 5% of women access

---

[4] RED Di Tella font based on EPH-INDEC

[5] RED Di Tella font based on EPH-INDEC

CEO or General Manager positions.[6]

But in addition to the statistical numbers, we must add to the analysis of the context, beliefs or prejudices, about preconceived ideas of what women are like, what we can and cannot do.

And up to this point, after the objective information provided by the statistics, I cannot help but give my subjective opinion on the subject, based on my experience and also great information gathered from many different leaders, with whom I had commercial, work, and professional relationships or simply had the opportunity to meet. In this sense, it is worth noting that, although women have a different leadership style, it is neither better nor worse than that of men, although in organizations in general it is dismissed because it is seen as less effective only because other aspects are valued more.

This is why it seems vital to me to distinguish, value and defend the different leadership styles, where the woman's style provides a differential value that organizations cannot afford to reject,

---

[6] Fuente Grant Thornton (2017)

and that women must learn to defend and highlight and not fall into copying models that have become obsolete or are foreign to us.

Stereotypes are mental models that limit the work and personal development of both women and men inside and outside organizations.

New models are needed, new ideas that allow us to create truly inclusive spaces, where within the different aspects of diversity, gender is the first chapter.

It is about integrating, integrating men and women, I do not even dare to invite us to merge since the important thing is not to lose the wealth that each of the parties brings.

What are the obstacles that women face?

Basically, women encounter 3 types of obstacles in their development, two of them are exogenous or variables external to us and one is endogenous or internal:

1. **Structural or cultural obstacles.** Within this first group we find:

- Discrimination against women, since it is an androcentric world, where the gaze places the man in the center and the woman is relegated, subordinated to the man, which shows that we definitely develop in a discriminatory society.

- The sexual division of labor that translates into the assignment of work functions and tasks according to gender, thus the man is assigned to the productive sphere and the woman to the reproductive sphere. This division of roles, where one becomes the productive, the leader, the generator, the provider and the other is relegated to the internal and loving tasks of assistance, cleaning and care, gives rise to the hierarchization that makes him at a neuralgic point in terms of the power asymmetries that are generated.

- The sexual division that translates into gender roles within homes, generating an unequal allocation of unpaid tasks that fall on women.

2. Organizational obstacles.

Within this group we can mention:

- The mirage of equality, where it is believed that they are in good gender since there is an equal or greater percentage of women than men, what it does not show is that they are all occupying positions at the base and when they go up the pyramid, women's participation falls drastically.

- The famous glass ceiling, which is the veiled limitation on women's career advancement to occupy leadership positions in top management. It is a ceiling that limits their professional careers, is difficult to overcome and prevents further progress.

- The not so famous, but common glass wall syndrome that consists of women being pigeonholed into certain roles, which can lead to management positions, but which do not allow them to advance beyond that level of the organization, such as human resources, institutional relations or corporate social responsibility.

269

- The prioritization of male management and leadership styles, where organizations, created by men, prioritize this model of management and leadership.

- Availability and full mobility in men, where men are the ones who are 100% available to attend to commitments such as business dinners, sports championships or recurring trips, while women are more reserved for the home environment.

- Gender-biased corporate policies that fuel differences in this aspect.

- The invisibility of leading women leaders.

3. Personal obstacles.

In general, these are limiting beliefs on the part of women, among which I can mention:

- Lack of confidence, which generates a significant gap with respect to the male gender.

- Fear of success.

- Great difficulty in recognizing one's own

performance.

- Considering yourself less capable than men.

- A need to demonstrate your capabilities with more work.

- The development of a great feeling of guilt.

- Less development of protagonist positions.

- Lack of decision not to access development opportunities.

- Lack of courage.

- Not joining the club where decisions are made.

- Do not have the same or similar level of ambition in men.

- Avoid challenging positions that expose them to conflict.

- Difficulty reconciling work life with private life.

What actions are women doing?

In recent years, fortunately, there have been advances by women to gain ground in these places, although not at the pace or speed that I would like, but at least there are no plateaus or setbacks. This is how you can see that women have started:

- To raise awareness among men about various difficulties.

- To show that they can occupy high positions without falling into masculinization.

- To promote women in challenging positions.

- To encourage ambition to counteract self-limitation.

- To provoke the generation of organizational policies that promote gender equality.

- To develop mentoring programs.

Leadership, art or science?

Definitely, leadership is not an exact science since it is about people and we do not all react the

272

same way, this confirms that leading is an art where the leader adapts to the team, seeking to influence people so that they generate the desired results, without neglecting one's own goals; to lead is to excite, it is to infect, it is to motivate, to lead is to develop, it is to provide vision, support, supervision, guidance, it is to show the way and set an example.

Although the new generations are bringing and will continue to bring gender equality in different areas, public and private, there is still a long way to go, where all work that can be done in this field will provide benefits in every sense.

The brilliant Peter Druker already said it, "The excellence of a leader is measured by the ability to transform problems into opportunities" and who else but us women know about that? When on the path we have to travel in life we encounter problems that we solve more simply, creatively and quickly than many men.

But again, it's not about them or us, it's about both and it's about harmonizing and complementing each other with the best that both styles bring. Now either way, it's always about art.

Our contribution

I am not a sexist, nor a feminist, I love diversity, in my work teams I really enjoy working with both women and men, I love how we complement each other and how we contribute to each other.

Men provide focus, determination, risk-taking, we provide empathy, analytical skills, planning, organization, our sixth sense, multitasking, among other things.

Even neuroscience explains some cognitive advantages that women's brain structure provides, such as the prefrontal cortex, the brain area in charge of higher connective and executive connections. It is what regulates everything that has to do with planning, decision making and problem solving, and studies indicate that women clearly have it much more developed than men. Just as it was studied that Einstein's was more developed than the rest of human beings.

On the other hand, it is full of statistics

worldwide, but among the main ones that I can mention is that of the ILO, which measures the existing gap in the active labor force, in the level of unemployment and the salary difference, between the indicators more relevant. Meanwhile The World Economic Forum measures and studies, among others, the GAP that exists between men and women in various aspects such as politics, education and economics, in addition to measuring the difference that exists in occupying management positions. The results, show an improvement in the treatment of these differences in recent years and with some of these gaps practically closed, such as the training aspects, where it will be balanced in just 12 years, which turns out to be a relatively early future. But in the economic aspect, closing these gaps in some cases will require 257 years, that is, neither our children, nor our grandchildren, nor great-grandchildren will see it, and although this seems extremely discouraging, we must continue working to ensure that this change does not continue to be delayed.

On the other hand, there are studies that indicate that the increase in the workforce of women, especially in management positions, allows

276

improving the sustainable results of companies, that is, not only considering the economic aspect, but also caring for the environmental and social development.

Additionally, it is proven that the increase in women in executive positions improves all the ratios of the companies that have put it into practice.

Finally, economic equality between men and women would allow an 11% increase in the Gross World Product.[7]

This world has room for both of us, it's just that they knew how to occupy it and we didn't. Until now...

A leader is not born, A leader is made!

I start from the basis, which is that a leader must have many characteristics and skills, which in some cases may be innate and may be easier to apply, but what I want to make absolutely clear is that all of these skills can be learned and developed, that is

---

[7] Source: Kinsey Institute

why the most important thing is the decision, determination, perseverance, attitude and perseverance to achieve it.

Of course, you can be a leader and boss at times, when? When the situation really calls for being a manager, but what is not possible is the other way around, just as MasterCard advertising mentions: "there are things that money cannot buy", it is said that leadership is not bought by the power a position grants.

Therefore, my invitation in this book, is to take you to the place of protagonists and put you into action!

We have already talked about the famous *stoppers*, which by working on them fully enable us to develop places of decision.

I have also developed, conceptually and experientially, the 12 fundamental skills that you should carry in your suitcase to begin moving into a leadership role; while also leaving a series of reflective questions for you to work on your self-diagnosis and invite you to reflect on the topic developed to take a qualitative and quantitative leap that allows you to reach your goal.

278

Now it's time to go out on the field! To play your game.

The place that I always recommend you take is that of the protagonist, that is the place that will allow you to act and advance, since the role of victim paralyzes you, flattens you and does not give you any benefit other than that of easily consoling yourself for not achieving the proposed results.

Furthermore, of all the barriers that we mentioned, which are present in the development of female leadership, the ones we can draw on are the personal barriers, since neither the cultural nor the organizational barriers depend directly on us.

So, with that said, the first thing I recommend doing is starting with self-leadership, because if I ask you: who is the most difficult person to lead in this world? The answer is not the elderly maintenance man, nor the owner's daughter, the correct answer is oneself. And although the answer is not difficult, achieving it is what is very complex, but… absolutely necessary since every good leader must predominate:

- *Coherence*: which should never lead me to ask for something that I am not or that I

279

would never do.

- **Values:** that give us the basis of principles, virtues and qualities that characterize us as a person, which are typically considered positive or of great importance by a social group.

- **Vision:** It is the fundamental quality of the leader and, to describe it well, I am going to bring the passage from a fable that I love and that talks about 3 bricklayers where, when the first one is asked what he's doing, he answers that he is laying bricks. The second, when asked the same question, mentions that he is building a wall and the third, when faced with the same question and situation, responds that he is building a university, the first in the town that his son and the next generations of young people and children will attend.

- **Commitment:** with oneself, the team and the personal and project goals.

- **Respect:** for oneself and for the rest of the individuals with whom I interact in the different roles of my life.

- *Responsibility*: about my actions, taking care of the decisions I make, carrying out behaviors that seek to improve oneself and help others.

- *Being on time:* which speaks of respect for my time and other people's time.

- *Assertive communication*: with the ability to adequately communicate the message you want to convey, developing an excellent level of listening and empathy.

- *Charisma:* that allows you to generate attraction in others. Here it is important that you know that charismatic personalities can be trained by staying alert and developing self-esteem, avoiding stress, mastering body language, developing the expression of the eyes and hands, not complaining and reproducing kind words.

- *Attitude*: it is the mood with which we approach a certain situation, it can be negative or positive, and this is definitely the key, not only in leadership but in life. Of course, when we refer to attitude, we do so in relation to having a positive attitude, the attitude that makes you feel like you can take on the world!

After self-leadership or your personal leadership, you go up to the next step, which is about working on interpersonal leadership, which is neither more nor less than one-on-one leadership, which can be with a colleague, a direct report, or a matrix one (more difficult), with a professional who provides external services and even with your boss.

The next step is team leadership, where you can lead different personalities, different backgrounds, different cultures, different sexes, different ages, different seniorities, where articulating the achievement of goals in harmony is the very art of leading.

Finally, it is about leading multiple teams, which come together in an organization, with their own goals aligned to the main one, it is the last step in the leadership phases.

This is how in the evolution of a leader, it is first about dedicating themselves to carry out the tasks and functions of their role, and after passing this stage, they begin to manage the tasks of others and finally prepares to lead other people with personal goals, team and organizational, where the art is to align them and make them all work well and in an articulated way.

On the path of leadership, I invite you to develop empowerment, which means "having the power to" which is fundamental to taking the key that opens the doors on your path.

They must also develop a good level of self-esteem, where, although parents play a fundamental role, there are instances where we can do everything necessary and make self-esteem work, with empathy, listening and a lot of work and perseverance.

Now, it is essential that you seek to carry the flame, which is basically generated by some central mobilizer in your life, in general this can be the hunger to achieve something that you did not have or the thirst for glory or altruism that allows you to dream and work for a better world.

Thus, you must go in search of the explosion produced by having the development of the skills of heart, brain, and courage, and the fuel to be able to decide, sell, negotiate, manage finances, develop networks with coherence, without feeling guilt, dynamiting glass ceilings, with the determination to occupy the place you want to occupy, without fear of making a mistake!

Always remember something! The great athletes who have achieved records are united by a secret: "they are not afraid to make mistakes", they see error as a possible result and nothing more. So is that Kobe Bryant, to his record for most missed shots, said "I don't care." The Lakers guard was the player who has missed the most shots in NBA history.

Reaching high has a price: you must try everything, many actions will go outside the arc, but never be afraid to err since fear is wise, it matters to us, and it affects us. But knowing how to live and coexist with the fear of making mistakes is the key. Live fully, know how to impose yourself, don't say yes to everything, don't fear rejection or starting over. Contrary to what common sense says, that risking losing is important, I believe... that risking not to win is the flame that must be carried.

Why try it? Precisely for that, so as not to be afraid to make mistakes and leave the best of ourselves! There is always learning, which will not exist unless you try. So is that the most successful athletes always get angry with those who don't try, but no one gets angry with those who try.

Trying is the flame!

Trying is making the effort and steps necessary to do something or achieve a certain objective or goal, without being absolutely certain of achieving it.

Trying without certainty precisely produces the certainty necessary to move forward.

Go out on the court and sweat your shirt! Go conquer that place that is for you!

Put all the passion, a dose of courage, the knowledge you have accumulated and the attitude you have and whatever you get out there too! And, believe me, at most you will make a mistake the first or second time, but with perseverance, resilience and a good guide, there is no way you won't succeed =).

Some tips for leading

- *Take advantage of feminine qualities:* they are those culturally associated with women. Empathy, kindness, compassion, perseverance, which are not associated with traditional leadership, but are essential for good leaders in an increasingly connected world.

- *Be authentic:* Don't hide who you are in order to occupy places that have male models.

- *Align corporate values with personal values:* Working for a purpose that doesn't fit with your own is always exhausting.

- *Share your story:* Leaders have a story of how they did it. That brings the teams closer. In the case of women even more so. Be generous and share how you managed to get to the place where you are and where you intend to be.

- ***Unfold your vision by focusing on the big picture:*** Keeping goals in mind helps lower the pressure.

- ***Develop your courage:*** Move and leave your comfort zone to get into action! Only by taking a deep breath and trying again and again will you cross the line of fear and achieve success.

- ***Let's raise our hands:*** This means that in addition to expecting leaders to notice our own skills, competencies and results, we should be the ones asking for the projects we want to lead.

Immediate actions to do

✓ Look for mentors who will accompany us in the long term.

✓ Writing a book helps organize ideas.

✓ Understand the problems we can solve, please be specific and accurate.

✓ Analyze how to develop links.

✓ Always act with transparency and consistency.

✓ Let dreams become reality.

Some phrases to treasure

"No one can make you feel inferior, without your consent."
ELEANOR ROOSEVELT

"I don't want women to have power over men, but over themselves."
MARY WOLLSTONECRAFT

"If you let your fears out you will have more space to live your dreams."
MARILYN MONROE

"If you want different results, do not do the same things."
ALBERT EINSTEIN

After reading the entire book, I invite you to let each of these phrases become the trigger for a new path and a new woman, which allows you to build a self-esteem so strong that no one can make you feel inferior; an empowerment that gives you the necessary power to do everything you set your mind to, with fewer fears and many more dreams.

You read me correctly, I am inviting you to build your new life, which one? The one you want, the one you dream of, the one that you thought a thousand times was for others... and today you are here, with my book in your hands, which came for a reason: to give you the opportunity to occupy that place and train yourself for it!

How to start?

Doing!

Start now!

Write to me and contact me on LinkedIn to incorporate this methodology into your organization.

Piñeiro's Methodology of Skills and Enablers

How?

The skill, experience, focus and boldness of a mentor determines the "peers" to develop in each executive, and how to develop "peers" in middle management.

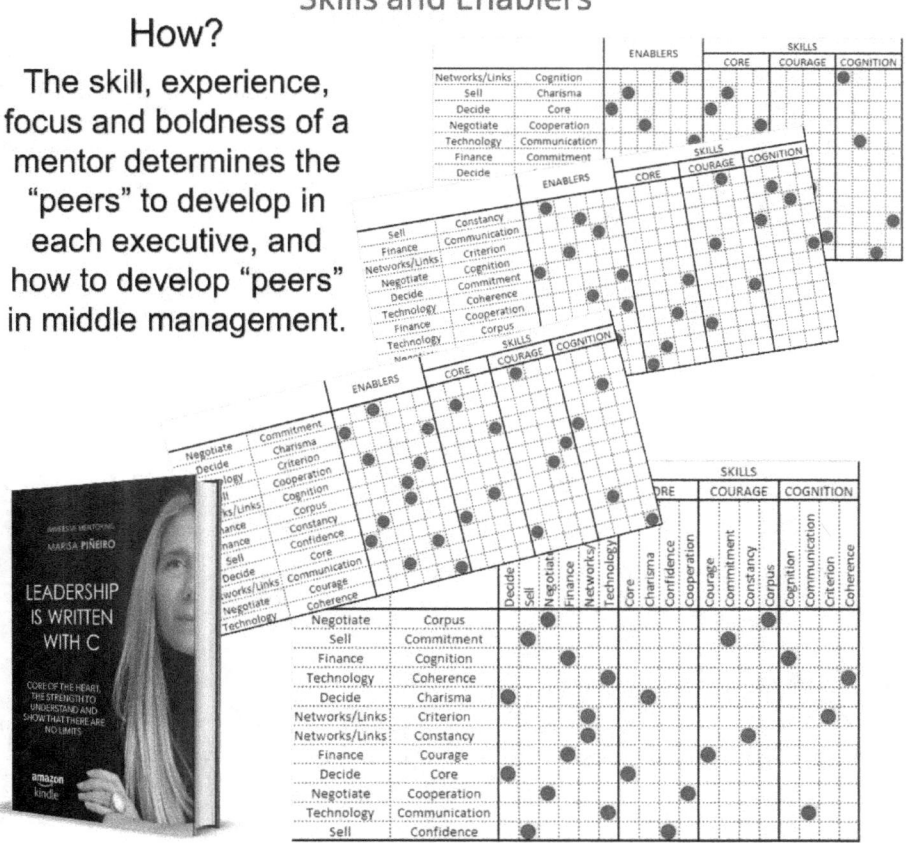

MARISA PIÑEIRO BIOGRAPHY

https://www.linkedin.com/in/marisaPiñeiro

Executive with vast experience in the local and international media industry.

- She has led important multinational companies, carried out large processes of *startup* and major restructurings.
- She gave international conferences on topics related to her field of expertise.
- She has successfully implemented Compliance programs.
- She has developed and implemented Strategic Planning and BSC methodology.
- She has created and implemented a sustainable media management strategy.
- She participated in the transformation of public media management by playing the role of Human Resources Director of RTA SE, a Public Media

293

group that is made up of Public Television and National Radio, with its 49 stations distributed throughout the country, with a staff of 3,000 employees at the beginning of the administration, in addition to advising Télam state news agency and Minister Hernán Lombardi, in charge of the Public Media system.

- She participated in different mentoring projects for professional women, both corporate and entrepreneurial, and is part of several organizations that work on the development and empowerment of women, such as:
  - o Vital Voices
  - o All Ladies League
  - o World Economic Forum
  - o Women Leaders
  - o ISFP
  - o FAME
- During 2020, she is presiding over the Argentine chapter of CERTAL Center for Regulatory Studies for the Development of Telecommunications and Access to the Information Society in Latin America.
- She is the creator of a Forum of Women Leaders in Latin America, which she called 'Mujeres en Positivo', which purpose is to work on the

294

empowerment, development, entrepreneurship, equity and visibility of women and their abilities.

- She has also created and developed the idea and general production of the program that will be one of the communication channels of this Forum, where different leaders from the field of politics, education, business, culture, entrepreneurship and social organizations in Latin America will be interviewed.

Academic training

Regarding her academic training, Marisa is a National Public Accountant and has a degree in Administration - UNLZ (1996), distinguished with a gold medal and special mention for an academic grade of 8.9.

From her executive training, are mentioned:

- Strategic Master in Human Resources Management - UCES (2005).

- PDD – Management Development Program – IAE (2011)

- PERH – Executive People Management Program – IAE (2009)

- Postgraduate in Management – UB (2006)

Postgraduate in Labor Legislation – USAL (2000)

www.ingramcontent.com/pod-product-compliance
Lightning Source LLC
Chambersburg PA
CBHW072353290526
45794CB00001B/59